"Increasingly readers of the Bible are wondering aloud how they are to deal with such moral problems as the apparent divine approval of slavery and genocide. In this volume Kent Sparks invites Christians of whatever theological persuasion to engage with Scripture as God's authoritative Word. He voices his own problems with the 'hard texts,' warns against trivializing them, and looks for a possible positive way forward. This is a book to be taken seriously and read sympathetically, for the problems discussed are very real, and a candid conversation about them must be allowed to take place if Christians are to speak credibly in the contemporary world."

— I. HOWARD MARSHALL
University of Aberdeen

"In clear prose reflecting his deep reading, Kent Sparks delivers an approach to Scripture that is driven by his unstinting attention to the most troubling and disturbing texts in the Bible. This careful and thoughtful investigation is designed to bring Christian students face to face with 'texts of terror' and to provide them with theological resources for moving forward in faith and with integrity."

— STEPHEN FOWL
Loyola University Maryland

SACRED WORD, BROKEN WORD

Biblical Authority and the Dark Side of Scripture

Kenton L. Sparks

William B. Eerdmans Publishing Company

Grand Rapids, Michigan / Cambridge, U.K.

Published 2012 by
Wm. B. Eerdmans Publishing Co.
2140 Oak Industrial Drive N.E., Grand Rapids, Michigan 49505 /
P.O. Box 163, Cambridge CB3 9PU U.K.

Printed in the United States of America

17 16 15 14 13 12   7 6 5 4 3 2 1

Library of Congress Cataloging-in-Publication Data

Sparks, Kenton L.
Sacred word, broken word: biblical authority and the dark side of Scripture /
Kenton L. Sparks.
p.   cm.
Includes indexes.
ISBN 978-0-8028-6718-6 (pbk.: alk. paper)
1. Bible — Hermeneutics.   2. Bible — Theology.   I. Title.

BS476.S68   2012
220.601 — dc23

2011039627

www.eerdmans.com

for Cheryl

Contents

CONTENTS

Abbreviations

AB	Anchor Bible
ACCS	Ancient Christian Commentary on Scripture
ANF	*Ante-Nicene Fathers*. Edited by A. Roberts and J. Donaldson. 10 vols. Reprint, Peabody, MA: Hendrickson, 1994.
BibSac	*Bibliotheca Sacra*
CBQ	*Catholic Biblical Quarterly*
ICC	International Critical Commentary
JETS	*Journal of the Evangelical Theological Society*
JTI	*Journal of Theological Interpretation*
LCL	Loeb Classical Library
LXX	Greek Septuagint
MAL	Middle Assyrian Laws
NCBC	New Century Bible Commentary
NIV	New International Version
NPNF1	*Nicene and Post-Nicene Fathers*, Series 1. Edited by P. Schaff. 14 vols. Reprint, Peabody, MA: Hendrickson, 1994.
NPNF2	*Nicene and Post-Nicene Fathers*, Series 2. Edited by P. Schaff and H. Wace. 14 vols. Reprint, Peabody, MA: Hendrickson, 1994.
NRSV	New Revised Standard Version
RelStud	*Religious Studies*
RSV	Revised Standard Version
SBLWAW	Society of Biblical Literature Writings of the Ancient World
SBT2	Studies in Biblical Theology, Second Series

TDOT	*Theological Dictionary of the Old Testament.* Edited by G. J. Botterweck, H. Ringgren, and H.-J. Fabry. 17 vols. Grand Rapids, MI: Eerdmans, 1974-.
ThTo	*Theology Today*
TSF Bulletin	*Theological Students Fellowship Bulletin*
WUNT	Wissenschaftliche Untersuchungen zum Neuen Testament

Preface

Numerous readers of my earlier book, *God's Word in Human Words*, have requested that I write a shorter and more focused book suitable as a supplemental text for college and seminary classes. The result is *Sacred Word, Broken Word*. In comparison with the earlier book, this one is less entangled with the special issues and concerns of Evangelical Christians and stands more directly within the emerging genre of ecumenical books on the subject of "Theological Interpretation."

Theological Interpretation is a hermeneutical movement that has surfaced in the last few decades. During the 1960s, intellectual developments that began during the Enlightenment finally culminated in the rise of "Biblical Studies," a new discipline that studied the Bible from a historical rather than theological point of view. Biblical scholars thus tended to abandon theology, and theologians, in response, and for other reasons, tended to abandon Scripture. The result was a methodological fracture between biblical and theological studies. The Theological Interpretation movement seeks to heal this breach by bringing the two traditions of discourse — Bible and theology — back together again. Miroslav Volf has characterized this as "the most significant theological development in the last two decades."[1] Whether this is the case or not, the movement is

---

1. Miroslav Volf, *Captive to the Word of God: Engaging the Scriptures for Contemporary Theological Reflection* (Grand Rapids: Eerdmans, 2010), 14.

exciting, and I am pleased to contribute modestly to this new theological work.

Insofar as possible, I avoid taking specific positions on matters that do not bear directly on my theological theme. This is not for lack of theological opinions; rather, it reflects the fact that biblical interpretation already entails more than enough to squabble about. Also, I think that from time to time it is heuristically beneficial to revisit our approach to Scripture before we return to hotly contended theological issues.

Behind this book stand many benefactors. Among my colleagues at Eastern University I would especially mention Steve Boyer, Phil Cary, Caroline Cherry, Eric Flett, Betsy Morgan, Carl Mosser, R. J. Snell, Ray Van Leeuwen, and Jonathan Yonan. All of them are kind, bright, and thoughtful colleagues. Among those from other institutions and places, I would single out Pete Enns (Biologos Foundation), Stephen Fowl (Loyola College), Eric Seibert (Messiah College), John Webster (University of Aberdeen), and David Vinson (Kaiser Permanente), who each worked through all or part of the manuscript and offered valuable suggestions. Countless others, too numerous to name, have also provided beneficial comments. To one and all, I offer a sincere word of thanks.

I dedicate this book to my wife Cheryl. She is an extraordinary blessing from God to everyone her life touches. By expertise both a health care and mental health professional, she has seen as much as anyone just how broken human beings can be — from the burn patient covered with open wounds to the schizophrenic on the therapy couch, the variety and depth of human suffering seems limitless. Yet she knows, too, that these extreme examples of brokenness and pain — physical, psychological, and spiritual — are reminders that all of us are broken people, who stand in desperate need of what Christ offers. I hope that this little book honors her belief that God can and does use broken people to bring healing to the lives of broken neighbors.

Soli deo Gloria!

We must read this book of books with all human methods. But through the fragile and broken Bible, God meets us in the voice of the Risen One.

Dietrich Bonhoeffer, *Reflections on the Bible*

First Thoughts

This is a book written for confessing Christians. Readers who are not Christians but are interested in the faith, either because they contemplate converting to it or are simply curious about it, may well find something useful in these pages; in fact, I hope that they do. But again, this is really a book for Christians. In saying this, I mean to say as well that this is an ecumenical book — that it is not for a particular group of Christians but rather for believers of every stripe, for Catholics, Protestants, and Orthodox, and for Liberals, Moderates, and Conservatives. It is also for those who, for some reason or other, try to avoid these kinds of labels when identifying themselves as "Christian."

Because this is a book for Christians, my discussion will assume the basic legitimacy and cogency of traditional Christian orthodoxy. That God exists and is good, that Jesus Christ is God incarnate, that the Bible is the word of God and hence authoritative for Christians, that there are such things as orthodoxy (right religious beliefs) and heresy (wrong religious beliefs) — all of these are matters of dogmatic theology that I will treat as finally settled. But an affirmation of basic Christian orthodoxy does not preclude theological disagreement. There are hundreds of Christian traditions, each with somewhat different viewpoints — sometimes very different viewpoints — on the same questions and matters. Is the Eucharist symbol or substance? Is baptism a sign of faith or initiation into it? Is righteousness imputed or imparted? Is there such a thing as apostolic succession, and if so, of what sort and under what conditions? Should Christians play vital roles in civil government or no roles at all? Can women be ordained as pastors? Is the local church governed by bishops, by local elders, or by the congregation as a whole? Are the wills of Christians predestined to faith, or do they freely choose to believe? Will everyone who is not a Christian face God's wrath, or will some who are not Christians nonetheless be saved through Christ? Will everyone finally be saved? The list of questions and the different Christian answers to them are legion.

Now theological differences do not always signal theological error. It is possible that, judged from a God's-eye perspective, it is just as legitimate to govern a church by "elder rule" as by "congregational rule," or to baptize by sprinkling as by immersing in water. Perhaps in these and other cases, God's concern is that we choose a wise solution rather than a particular solution. At the same time, in the final analysis it seems clear, too, that not everyone can be right about everything. We cannot really affirm at the same time that the Eucharist is literally the body and blood of Christ (so Catholicism) *and* that it certainly is not the body and blood (so many Protestants). We cannot affirm that all unbelievers will be lost for eternity *and* that some or all of them will finally be saved. It really must be the case that, at some points, every branch and bough of the Christian tradition is getting something wrong. One implication is that any healthy Christian tradition does more than simply perpetuate its beliefs and practices from one generation to the next: it also interrogates that tradition, asking here and there whether the inherited tradition has it quite right.[1] Is there something that is believed and practiced in our particular wing or communion of the church that is wrong or unwise and, more importantly, that, because it is believed and practiced, does damage to the cause of faith itself?

To give just one example, let us consider Christian views of the cosmos. There was a time in church history when the acceptable view was that the earth stood at the center of the universe.[2] For centuries this Ptole-

1. For an argument that healthy traditions are able to interrogate their own boundaries, see Alasdair MacIntyre, *Whose Justice? Which Rationality?* (Notre Dame, IN: University of Notre Dame Press, 1988).

2. See Giorgio de Santillana, *The Crime of Galileo* (Chicago: University of Chicago Press, 1955); Jerome J. Langford, *Galileo, Science, and the Church* (rev. ed.; Ann Arbor: University of Michigan, 1971); Thomas S. Kuhn, *The Copernican Revolution* (Cambridge: Harvard University,

maic perspective presented no problems, but eventually advances in science — led by men like Copernicus and Galileo — uncovered the problems in this view of astronomy. These scholars realized that the best explanation by far for what we could see in the sky was the heliocentric theory, according to which the sun, not the earth, stood at the center of our solar system. The church did not manage the situation very well. The book of Copernicus, *De Revolutionibus,* was banned to Catholic readers. As for Galileo, he was forced under threats to recant his views, as he and other like-minded scientists were accused of or charged with heresy. Though it is quite true that the church eventually accepted the new cosmological theories, its initial and clumsy response did significant damage to its reputation in intellectual circles. As Wolfhart Pannenberg has pointed out, a chasm began to develop between the church and the scientific community in those days, a chasm that has mainly grown wider as the years have gone by.[3]

From this example I would draw out two observations. First, we notice that mistaken Christian beliefs — like the geocentric cosmology — can survive for centuries without creating any serious problems for the church's life or witness. And second, in certain circumstances it comes about that long-held traditions, which previously created no particular problems, either gradually or suddenly begin to engender difficulties as advances in our understanding uncover errors in the tradition. So the church needs to be vigilant not only in guarding its tradition (something it has often done well) but also in carefully considering where that tradition might be mistaken (something it has often failed to do).

Here I would suggest, along with many others, that the time has come to reconsider carefully a particular matter of theology that has come to the fore in the modern age. The subject is Holy Scripture.[4] I believe that

---

1957); Friedel Weinert, *Copernicus, Darwin, and Freud: Revolutions in the History and Philosophy of Science* (Malden, MA: Wiley-Blackwell, 2009).

3. Wolfhart Pannenberg, "The Doctrine of Creation and Modern Science," *Zygon* 23 (1988): 3-21, here p. 4.

4. Dale Martin, in particular, has stressed that training in Scripture should begin with questions of theology and interpretive theory before plunging headlong into detailed readings of Scripture itself. See Dale B. Martin, *Pedagogy of the Bible: An Analysis and Proposal* (Louisville: Westminster John Knox, 2008).

within my American and Western theological context — and in other places deeply touched by it — we are in need of a fresh look at how Scripture is read and used as a theological resource for nourishing the church. Very conservative Christians — of whom there are many — tend to read Scripture with a rigidity and simplicity that rob it of its proper theological vitality, and very liberal Christians — of whom there are also many — tend to feel that Scripture's authority has been so undermined by modern and postmodern insight that it is of little, practical theological use. Between these two extremes one finds many religious people (who variously identify themselves as "moderates" or "post-liberals" or with some similar label) who are laboring to take Scripture seriously while admitting that doing theology is far more complicated than simply quoting the Bible. I suppose that in terms of approach and method my posture toward Scripture is closer to this moderate camp, though I would caution that these kinds of labels — conservative, moderate, and liberal — have little to do with the kind of Christian that one is. I know conservatives, moderates, and liberals who deeply love God and neighbor, as well as those sporting these labels that seem more challenged by these affections.

It will become clear that my discussion of Scripture has in its cross-hairs a particular theological difficulty. The "flash point" is not the usual suspect, by which I mean modern historical criticism and the ostensible tensions and contradictions that scholars have uncovered in the Bible. In my opinion Scripture's human errors, though relevant to interpretation, tend to be fairly innocuous theologically. Does it really matter how Judas died? Or how much King David paid for the temple site? Or whether Paul went to Jerusalem soon after his conversion or much later? Or how long Israel was enslaved in Egypt? That the Bible offers conflicting answers for these kinds of questions is of no surprise given that it was written by human beings who lived in diverse times and places. No, my immediate concern is not with error per se but, more specifically, with those biblical texts that one scholar has called "texts of terror."[5] How are Christians to understand Scripture when it directs God's people to slaughter Canaanite fami-

---

5. Phyllis Trible, *Texts of Terror: Literary-Feminist Readings of Biblical Narratives* (new ed.; London: SCM Press, 2002); cf. the recent and important book by Eric A. Seibert, *Disturbing Divine Behavior: Troubling Old Testament Images of God* (Minneapolis: Fortress, 2009).

lies — men, women, and children — merely because they have false religious beliefs that could unduly influence Israel? And what are we to do with the many biblical texts that explicitly or implicitly support slavery, sometimes permitting slave owners to beat slaves or to treat foreign slaves more harshly? And what of those texts that regard women as property or as second-class citizens, in some cases forbidding women to speak in public worship? One can easily make this list very long.

Just about every Christian I know is troubled by these biblical texts. It does not seem to matter much whether they sport a liberal or conservative label. The confusion is not something we talk about much, but my sense is that it is time to face up to it. For whether we like the sentiment or not, there are growing convictions among unbelievers, and even among Christians, that "something is rotten in Denmark."

As I offer my perspectives in this book, I do not intend to speak, I hope, as if I am the final arbiter of truth. My judgments on these matters could be wrong, and any of the views that I describe and critique may be far better than my own. But that said, I write because I believe there is something profitable that I can say when it comes to Scripture and how Christians read it. And, though this book is not an apologetic book, there is perhaps something of value in it for those who do not (yet!) share the Christian faith.

CHAPTER 1

The Truth and Beauty of Sacred Scripture

L et us begin on a high note, with Scripture's truth and beauty. The brevity of my discussion is not a function of its importance. It reflects instead my assumption that Scripture's appeal is self-evident to confessing Christians. No arguments are necessary. So I take up the theme of Scripture's beauty mainly to emphasize from the outset the underlying premise of our discussion. On the whole Scripture is a wonderful book, a divinely given book that powerfully witnesses to and participates in God's saving work in our cosmos. Much that is good and right in our western society, even among those who do not share the Christian faith or read the Bible, is ultimately a product of biblical and Christian influences.[1] To love God, your neighbor, and your enemies is a potent biblical message that has directly and indirectly transformed many people and cultures for the good. For twenty centuries people shaped by Christian Scripture have shared their love with, and rendered aid to, those who suffer in our world. It is also true that Christians have sometimes misused Scripture to justify evil and oppression (a matter that we will take up soon enough), but I do not believe that this should distract us from the plain facts. God's word has been a source of blessing for humanity.

---

1. I am reminded of Robert Wuthnow's sociological study that demonstrated a connection, even among non-Christians, between familiarity with the biblical story of the Good Samaritan and actual kindness toward others. See his *Acts of Compassion: Caring for Others and Helping Ourselves* (Princeton: Princeton University Press, 1991), 157-90.

Scripture's charm is not a function merely of the wise things that it says and the good deeds that it engenders, though all of this is praiseworthy. Scripture's goodness and beauty stem from its Trinitarian character and from the way that it advances our relationship with the Godhead. Foremost, Scripture demonstrates that God wishes to speak to us and, to some extent, that we wish to hear from him.[2] It is an overture of love from God the Father to humanity.

Scripture is also beautiful because of its vital connection to the Son, Jesus Christ, God's solution for all that ails humanity and the cosmos. Apart from Christ there would be no New Testament at all, and I suspect that the Hebrew Bible would have remained the narrowly Jewish book that it always was. Scripture is God's book that points to Christ. The Bible's authors describe in detail, through four different books, the sort of life that Jesus lived, the things he believed, and the various ways in which he demonstrated God's love for humanity. All four Gospels culminate with the shocking revelation that God the Son died for us, and that this death, and the victory won against it, was a victory won on our behalf. Here God demonstrates his power through a paradox that makes friends of enemies by dying for them. The remaining books of the New Testament tease out the implications of Christ's victory for everyday life and for the final chapter of the cosmic story.

Scripture is also the sword of the Spirit (Eph 6:17). The Spirit moved people to write Scripture (2 Pet 1:21) and continues to use the books they wrote to nourish Christian souls. The result is our unity with the Holy Trinity — with the Father, Son, and Spirit. The author of 2 Peter actually suggests that we become "participants of the divine nature." Whatever this means, Paul tells us that this relationship provides spiritual power to overcome the grip of sin in our lives (Rom 6:1-14). Whereas our natural inclinations mainly serve selfish purposes, Spirit-given inclinations bear good fruit and inspire love for God and neighbor. The Spirit's use of Scripture is indeed mysterious — I simply do not know how it works — but the Christian tradition affirms the result: that "the just requirement of the law" can be fulfilled by those who "walk not according to the flesh

---

2. Whether some or all humans are drawn to this grace is something that need not concern us here.

but according to the Spirit" (Rom 8:4). In sum, Scripture is a vital resource that guides people to Christ and that helps us become healthier people.

Abstract theological concepts are fundamental to Christian theology, but the best way to see and appreciate Scripture's beauty is to read it. Here are a few representative examples of Scripture's beauty from the Old and New Testaments:

> If you meet your enemy's ox or his ass going astray, you shall bring it back to him. If you see the ass of one who hates you lying under its burden, you shall refrain from leaving him with it, you shall help him to lift it up. (Exod 23:4-5)

> Greater love has no man than this, that a man lay down his life for his friends. (John 15:13)

> Blessed are the poor in spirit, for theirs is the kingdom of heaven. Blessed are those who mourn, for they shall be comforted. Blessed are the meek, for they shall inherit the earth. Blessed are those who hunger and thirst for righteousness, for they shall be satisfied. Blessed are the merciful, for they shall obtain mercy. Blessed are the pure in heart, for they shall see God. Blessed are the peacemakers, for they shall be called sons of God. (Matt 5:3-9)

> If I speak in the tongues of men and of angels, but have not love, I am a noisy gong or a clanging cymbal. . . . Love is patient and kind; love is not jealous or boastful; it is not arrogant or rude. Love does not insist on its own way; it is not irritable or resentful; it does not rejoice at wrong, but rejoices in the right. Love bears all things, believes all things, hopes all things, endures all things. Love never ends. (1 Cor 13:1-8)

> But the fruit of the Spirit is love, joy, peace, patience, kindness, goodness, faithfulness, gentleness, self-control; against such there is no law. (Gal 5:22-23)

Paul was certainly right. No reasonable law could be forged to prohibit these kinds of virtues. The Bible simply *is* a beautiful book, and it has influenced the church and our world for the good.

In spite of Scripture's truth and beauty — which I take to be *obvious* — the clamor leveled against the Bible has increased markedly during the last decade. More and more critics argue that the Bible is a book of genocide, misogyny, child abuse, and slavery, a violent book that has inspired religious wars and persecution for centuries on end. Even some Christians have joined this throng, essentially throwing the Bible under the proverbial bus in the name of love and cultural relevance. While I certainly understand the reflex behind these responses to some parts of Scripture, it is overreaching, I think, to paint the whole of Scripture with one brush. Paradoxically, I will eventually argue that this critique of Scripture was inspired by Scripture itself. That is, Scripture is good, not only because it offers what is good, but also because it provides the remedy for where it is not so good.

If this is right, then it seems to me that Christians should approach Scripture with a hermeneutic of respect rather than suspicion. The Bible is not a nasty book containing a few misplaced nuggets of morality. It is a great and holy book that admittedly includes many unsavory elements. In the pages that follow, we will consider Scripture's peculiar difficulties with a spirit of respect for the written word and for the God who has given it to us.

CHAPTER 2

Creation and the Problem of Evil

Though our topic is Scripture, I would prefer to begin with creation, with the cosmos and the natural order, with the panoply of the heavens — sun, moon, stars, and distant galaxies that modern scientists have begun to lay bare for us, with the seemingly endless variety of flora and fauna on the earth, in the skies, and in the seas, and with that strangest of all species, which is aware of itself and contemplates its own life and death: humanity. There is no *necessary* reason why a book on Scripture should begin with a discussion of creation and its creatures. We could begin in many different places, including of course with Scripture itself. But I chose to begin with the created order for two reasons. First, the created order is historically prior to Scripture. It was and is the home of all people, of every race and creed, who have been born, lived, and died. Many of these people lived and died before Scripture was written, and still others have lived and died after the advent of Scripture but have, nonetheless, either never read it or have only passing familiarity with it. Apart from this human context, there would be no Scripture, for Scripture was written by and for human beings; creation is the larger *context* that makes the *text* of Scripture sensible.

Another reason for granting priority to creation is that Scripture itself highlights the priority of creation. It is on the testimony of the natural order, says Scripture, that people first believe in God and seek him out (cf. Romans 1). The apostle Paul (as reported by Luke) put it this way:

The God who made the world and everything in it, he who is Lord of heaven and earth, does not live in shrines made by human hands. . . . From one ancestor he made all nations to inhabit the whole earth, and he allotted the times of their existence and the boundaries of the places where they would live, so that they would search for God and perhaps grope for him and find him — though indeed he is not far from each one of us. For "In him we live and move and have our being"; as even some of your own poets have said, "For we too are his offspring." (Acts 17:24-28)

Certainly this search for God yields theological confusion to some degree or other, but *that* there can be a real grasping after God through the medium of the created order without the aid of Scripture (but presumably with the aid of divine grace) is affirmed by Scripture and the Christian tradition. When faith in God takes form in us, it is always in the context of our *prior* encounter with creation. Yet this encounter with the cosmos does not always produce faith and, paradoxically, sometimes seems to damage the prospect of faith. Whether it does damage depends in part on our answer to an important question.

The Perennial Problem of Evil and Suffering

Einstein said, "I think the most important question facing humanity is, 'Is the universe a friendly place?'"[1] I do not know if this is the most important question we face, but it is obviously very important and, perhaps, really is *the* fundamental question posed by human existence. The question arises because human experience offers disjointed and confusing evidence about the world we live in. Love, goodness, truth, and beauty affirm that the universe is friendly, but hatred, evil, falsehood, and pain suggest that it is not. Here I refer, of course, to perennial questions about "the problem of pain" or "the problem of evil." People respond differently to the problem and draw different conclusions from the evidence.

Anyone who has spent time with those who are not Christians will

1. E. Edward Bittar, *Bioethics* (Greenwich, CT: JAI Press, 1994), 159.

know that many among them simply cannot believe in a friendly universe nor, of course, in a friendly God.[2] From the gas chambers of Auschwitz to the genocide of Rwanda, from the famine of Calcutta's slums to the child with cancer, from the ever-present specter of war to the ubiquity of human poverty, the profundity of human suffering shows them that the cosmos was not made by a good God. "A good God would create a good universe," they say, "and in many respects the universe is not good."

Though I am a Christian, I freely confess that on a bad day this assessment of the human predicament resonates with me. After listening to particularly disturbing news reports (just yesterday 200,000 souls were lost when an earthquake devastated the poor Haitian city of Port-au-Prince) or after facing an exasperating day of my own, I sometimes find myself thinking, "If I were God, I would put a stop to that! God! Where the hell are you?" So the cynical logic of atheism makes some sense to me; evil readily suggests that the cosmos is not the work of, nor under the watchful eye of, a good and loving God.

Those who believe in God have tried to "solve" the problem of pain in different ways. One ancient solution, posited by the Gnostics, viewed the cosmos as the warped creation of an evil, inferior deity. Thus the superior God of love and wisdom was absolved of blame for the world's corruption. A more contemporary solution holds that God is good but not all-powerful and so cannot wholly impede evil's reign of terror. The Jewish rabbi Harold Kushner makes this argument in his best-selling book *When Bad Things Happen to Good People*.[3] Another solution actually denies that evil exists at all. Christian Scientists are perhaps the best-known Western advo-

---

2. For recent semi-popular examples, see Bart D. Ehrman, *God's Problem: How the Bible Fails to Answer Our Most Important Question — Why We Suffer* (New York: HarperOne, 2008); Christopher Hitchens, *God Is Not Great: How Religion Poisons Everything* (New York: Hachette, 2007). For more sophisticated philosophical arguments in this direction, see the articles by Hume, Mackie, Schellenberg, Draper, and Rowe in William L. Rowe, ed., *God and the Problem of Evil* (Malden, MA: Blackwell, 2001). See also Rowe's article, "The Problem of Evil and Some Varieties of Atheism," *American Philosophical Quarterly* 16 (1979): 335-41.

3. Harold S. Kushner, *When Bad Things Happen to Good People* (New York: Schocken Books, 1981). "Process Theologians" like Charles Hartshorne and John Cobb offer a more nuanced version of this thesis (see Kenneth Surin, *Theology and the Problem of Evil* [Oxford: Blackwell, 1986], 86-92).

cates of this viewpoint, which holds that all pain and suffering is an "illusion" that we can overcome by faith.[4] But in the end, Christian orthodoxy is not satisfied with these answers. On the matter of God and evil, we believe that atheists, Gnostics, Christian Scientists, and Rabbi Kushner are wrong.

The Christian tradition affirms that the cosmos is God's good and profoundly beautiful creation, but it is also "fallen" because our world is marred and warped by the effects of human sin.[5] This is an important element of the Christian *theodicy:* humanity, not God, is to blame for what ills the world.

As readers may know, the Christian tradition has generally maintained that human sin has negatively affected not only humanity but also the cosmos itself. The view is in part drawn from Genesis 3:14-19, but the influential voice is probably the apostle Paul, who expressed it this way:

> For the creation was subjected to futility, not of its own will but by the will of the one who subjected it, in hope that the creation itself will be set free from its bondage to decay and will obtain the freedom of the glory of the children of God. We know that the whole creation has been groaning in labor pains until now; and not only the creation, but we ourselves, who have the first fruits of the Spirit, groan inwardly while we wait for adoption, the redemption of our bodies. (Rom 8:20-23)[6]

Christian theologians over the course of history have essentially mimed this Pauline viewpoint,[7] which is nicely summed up in the Catholic Catechism:

4. The classic text is Mary Baker Eddy, *Science and Health with Key to the Scriptures* (Boston: Stewart, 1912). This approach to the problem is of course more common in Eastern religious philosophies.

5. Some modern scholars would like to modify this traditional language, often on the assumption that "the Fall" reflects Platonic categories foreign to Christian thought. As I use it here, the nomenclature merely refers to human sin and its negative effects in and on our world.

6. For other biblical texts that take physical evils seriously, see Mark 4:15 and, of course, the book of Job.

7. For examples ancient and modern, see John Chrysostom, *Homilies on Romans* 14 (NPNF1 11.444); Thomas Aquinas, *Summa Theologica* (5 vols.; Allen, TX: Christian Classics, 1981), 5.2853-62, especially 2860 (= supplement to part 3, q. 74); John Calvin, *Commentaries on*

Harmony with creation is broken: visible creation has become alien to man. Because of man, creation is now subject to "its bondage to decay."[8]

The basic point is that creation is a victim of human sin, which has led not only to war, genocide, poverty, and hunger but also to floods, droughts, disease, and death. Not only humanity, but the cosmos itself, stands in need of redemption. So the effects of the Fall are universal.

Some contemporary theologians would prefer to modify this traditional viewpoint by holding that humanity only, and not the natural order as a whole, is disordered. On this theory evil would entail only what is engendered by or directly associated with human sin.[9] Other unsavory events, such as human death by natural causes or animal death by tooth and fang, though unpleasant and sometimes painful, are not true evils. This modern perspective on evil is prompted by the scientific observation that life on earth has evolved through a continuous cycle of suffering and death. If we accept that this is the case, then it seems that we must follow one of two theological paths. We can follow the path blazed by Teilhard de Chardin, who viewed natural evils as the "growing pains" that give rise to greater goods,[10] or we must accept that ecosystems are not evil at all; they are integral to the very structure of God's beautiful cosmos.[11] But regardless of our choice here, one implication remains the same. The scientific

---

the First Book of Moses, called Genesis, tr. John King (2 vols.; Edinburgh: Calvin Translation Society, 1847-50), 1.177; T. F. Torrance, Divine and Contingent Order (Edinburgh: T. & T. Clark, 1981), 117.

8. See article III.400 in Catechism of the Catholic Church (Mahwah, NJ: Paulist Press, 1994), 101.

9. For examples, see Craig L. Nessan, "Christian Faith in Dialogue with Darwin: Evolutionary Biology and the Meaning of the Fall," Currents in Theology and Mission 29 (2002): 85-93; John Polkinghorne, Quarks, Chaos and Christianity (2nd ed.; New York: Crossroad, 2005). See also the discussion in Surin, Theology and the Problem of Evil, 60-64, 78-80.

10. Pierre Teilhard de Chardin, The Phenomenon of Man, tr. B. Wall (London: Collins, 1959).

11. This solution normally avers that we live in "the best of all possible worlds." For examples of this view, see Polkinghorne, Quarks, Chaos and Christianity; Christopher Southgate, The Groaning of Creation: God, Evolution, and the Problem of Evil (Louisville; London: Westminster John Knox, 2008); Peter van Inwagen, The Problem of Evil (Oxford: Clarendon Press, 2006).

evidence cannot square easily with the traditional view that human sin *caused* "natural evil" because animals existed and died long before humanity evolved. So we must speak now in terms of a "limited" rather than "universal" Fall, and our theological vocabulary should replace "natural evil" with tamer concepts, such as the "grief," "travail," or "groaning" of nature. This is the logic.

Theologians who advocate this "limited Fall" find ancient support in the writings of two church Fathers, Irenaeus and Augustine.[12] Irenaeus argued that, in contrast to human rebels, God's non-human creatures "persevered, and still persevere, in subjection to Him who formed them."[13] As for Augustine, he was always careful to interpret the Apostle Paul's comments about the Fall as pertaining to humanity only.[14] So it seems that neither Irenaeus nor Augustine was troubled by the natural state of the cosmos. We should of course take the views of Irenaeus and Augustine seriously, but we must keep in mind that both were engaged in lively debates with Gnostics who believed that the universe was the evil creation of an evil deity. It would have been much more difficult for Irenaeus and Augustine to defend their orthodox view of God as the creator of a good cosmos if they had admitted any disorders in nature, so I do not believe that their patristic judgments can be accepted at face value. Nonetheless, when it comes to the problems raised by animal suffering, their views do have certain advantages over the traditional viewpoint, as do the more nuanced and developed views advocated by some modern theologians.

As important as these questions are, it seems to me that the matter of "natural evil" is not something that I can address very well in a short book on Scripture. At this point I tend to side with the traditional view because I am (like some of the biblical authors) viscerally troubled by the suffering of beasts and because I suspect that, in the end, we will find it difficult to preserve a real separation between "nature" and human sin.[15] Some of the horrible things that humans do to each other can be chalked up, at least in

12. See H. Paul Santmire, *The Travail of Nature* (Philadelphia: Fortress, 1985), 31-73.

13. Irenaeus, *Against Heresies* 2.28.7 (ANF 1.401).

14. See Thomas E. Clarke, *The Eschatological Transformation of the Material World According to St. Augustine* (Woodstock, MD: Woodstock College Press, 1956), 34-35.

15. Gen 1:29-30; Isa 11:6; 65:25.

part, to natural dispositions rather than social formation and personal vo-
lition (see the footnote for possible implications). For this to work out
theologically, I would have to argue (it seems to me) that the cosmos
proleptically anticipated human sin. In essence, God created the world so
that the consequences of human sin were already in play before human
beings existed. There are indeed precedents for this idea in biblical, patristic, and modern thought.[16] But that said, I do not believe that this debate
dramatically affects what I have to say about Scripture. For my main point
is simply this: that God's creation — the good and beautiful thing that he
alone has made — entails evils monstrous and unspeakable, whether human only or human and natural together. As I will show, this basic theological affirmation provides an important analogy for our understanding
of Holy Scripture and its character.

How can we explain evil's presence in God's good creation without
implicating God as the author of evil? This question has come up from
time to time in church history, but only for modernity has it produced a
sustained theological and philosophical debate. As I have indicated already, the debate has generally been between Christians, who hold that
God is good in spite of evil's existence, and critics who believe that evil's
existence proves that God either is not good or, more usually, simply
does not exist. Christian scholars have usually advocated two kinds of
theodicy in response to the critics. One approach is theoretical. It attempts to offer intellectually satisfying arguments that defend God's
goodness in the face of evil. The other approach is more practical, in that
it confronts evil by pointing to and joining in God's effort to heal a broken, fallen world.[17] I believe that both kinds of theodicy have a role to
play in Christian responses to evil, though I side with Kenneth Surin's

16. The author of Genesis expressed this view in spatial terms, insofar as his created order included both an Edenic garden and the fallen world outside, prepared by God to receive
the rebellious human couple. Gregory of Nyssa and Augustine similarly argued that the created order already anticipated the Fall. For references and a sympathetic modern discussion,
see Marguerite Shuster, *The Fall and Sin: What We Have Become as Sinners* (Grand Rapids: Eerdmans, 2004), 77. Obviously, I am opposed to theories that trace cosmic trouble back to the
sins of angels or devils rather than humanity (for example, Alvin Plantinga, *God, Freedom, and
Evil* [Grand Rapids: Eerdmans, 1989]).

17. See the important discussion by Surin in *Theology and the Problem of Evil*.

opinion that the practical approach is foundational to any intellectual theodicies we can offer.[18]

Some theologians and philosophers are determined to *prove* that the Christian view of evil is right, but I do not believe that this is really possible. If we take the evil in our world seriously, we will find ourselves confronted by the specter of burning children, thrown alive into the furnaces at Auschwitz. Such unspeakable evil — one example from countless millions — inevitably engenders a debate like this one between two Jewish survivors of the holocaust:[19]

Gregor was angry. "After what happened to us, how can you believe in God?"

The Rabbi answered, "How can you *not* believe in God after what has happened?"

I do not believe that we should side with the rabbi too quickly. We must sympathize with Gregor's pain and anger and let the problem sink in. Anyone familiar with the books of Job and Ecclesiastes knows this. But in the end, I do think that we should agree with the rabbi. That is, without having proved our case, we *believe* as he did that it is more sensible to embrace the good God who stands against evil than to hold that the universe is either malevolent or indifferent to the fortunes of humanity.

But what of the obvious follow-up question? If the cosmos is *God's* creation, and if he is the "omnipotent" deity Christians say he is, how do Christians avoid implicating God in the evil and terror that befalls his world? Christians have erected and explicated a theological firewall between God and evil. While admitting that evil obviously exists in God's creation, Christians argue that responsibility for this cannot properly be traced back to God; it can only be traced back to human evil, back to the contrary position that *we* have taken up in opposition to God's goodness.

One implication of the foregoing is that good and evil are uncomfort-

18. See also William C. Placher's article, "Evil and Divine Transcendence," in his book *The Domestication of Transcendence* (Louisville: Westminster John Knox, 1996), 200-215.

19. A fictional conversation from Elie Wiesel's *The Gates of the Forest* (New York: Holt, Rinehart and Winston, 1970), 194.

ably juxtaposed in one creation. Imagine, if you will, a beautiful painting by the likes of Renoir or Monet. And then imagine that someone seizes it, rips it from the frame, crumples it up, and stomps on the painting for about ten minutes. What is left in the end? One has a beautiful painting that is everywhere warped and twisted. The former beauty of the unmolested painting is visible in some places more than others, but no quarter of the canvas has escaped the damage. This, I would say, suitably describes God's creation. Human beings are beautiful but also broken in a way that does not permit us to wholly separate what is beautiful from what is not. *Privation* is the technical theological term for this, according to which evil and disorder are always parasitic and never stand merely on their own.[20]

The Theological Message of a Warped World

Interpretation of the human situation therefore requires that we make prudent but difficult judgments about what ought to be in the natural order (what is good and properly ordered) and what should not have a part in it (what is evil and/or disordered). Scripture's own testimony reinforces this logic. Psalm 19 explicitly describes the created order as a "word" from God:

> The heavens are telling the glory of God;
>   and the firmament proclaims his handiwork.
> Day to day pours forth speech,
>   and night to night declares knowledge.
> There is no speech, nor are there words;
>   their voice is not heard.

(Ps 19:1-3)

The Bible further affirms (and this is a *very* important point) that *everything* in the created order — both good and bad — speaks a word from God.

---

20. The classic argument for privation was made by Augustine, though the view is now standard among Christians. For discussion, see R. Douglas Geivett, *Evil and the Evidence for God: The Challenge of John Hick's Theodicy* (Philadelphia: Temple University Press, 1993), 10-28.

This point is most poignantly advanced in the book of Proverbs. When the sages say, "Better a dry morsel with quiet than a house full of feasting with strife" (Prov 17:1), they teach truths that are derived from wisely observing both the good and ill of everyday life. That their insight from daily life constitutes a "word" from God is finally confirmed by its integration into canonical Scripture.

Though we are obliged to distinguish right from wrong and good from evil in the cosmos, I do not believe that there are fail-safe methods for making these judgments. The human condition is warped by the Fall, so careful sifting is required to distinguish God's original design from its distorted features. Moreover, our natural capacities to interpret the cosmos are also distorted; it is as if we are trying to view a warped world through warped glasses.

In spite of these difficulties, some moral judgments do seem fairly straightforward. There is a broad agreement among human beings, for example, that killing in "cold blood" violates the natural ethical order. But many other ethical decisions resist simple solutions. Should we or should we not use corporal discipline to teach our children? Should our justice system advocate capital punishment or rehabilitation? Shall we embrace "just wars" or pacifism? Should the poor be given housing and food, or should they fend for themselves as a consequence of their choices? Questions of this sort are difficult and numerous. Human beings have some capacity to make these evaluations and, to the extent that we are competent to do so, are culpable for how we make them. One thinks here of Paul's assertion that those without a Bible are responsible to the law "written on their hearts" (Rom 2:15).

Many Christians, especially very conservative Christians, believe that these ethical decisions are much less troublesome if we use the Bible as our guide. They are quite right about the advantage of having Scripture in hand, but Scripture does not guarantee good results. Our understanding of Scripture is never perfect, and we have even greater difficultly transcribing what we do understand into healthy, productive living. Yet there is another, equally important reason that Scripture does not resolve all of our questions.

The problem that I have in mind is *not* that the Bible addresses a limited number of issues and topics, nor the historical remoteness of its discourse, nor our propensity to misunderstand the Bible. Rather, one reason that the Bible is not a simple, straightforward "guide book" for life is that, as we shall see, the Bible actually stands *within* the fallen order that we seek to understand. That is, if I may foreshadow where I am heading in the discussion, *the problem of Scripture is one permutation of the larger problem of evil.*

This part of our discussion can be summarized as follows: (1) the created order is the good creation of a good God; (2) this good creation is fallen and includes evil and disorder; (3) human beings rather than God should be implicated for the troubling features of the created order; (4) because it is fallen, the created order stands in need of redemption; (5) because it is fallen, interpretation of the created order requires that we make judgments that distinguish what is good and fitting from what is evil and ill-fit for creation; (6) rendering these judgments is possible without consulting Scripture (apparently by "natural law") but facilitated when we *correctly* consult Scripture; (7) rendering these judgments requires a recognition that everything in the cosmos, both good and ill, speaks a word from God; and (8) the fact that our interpretations of the created order are not foolproof does not obviate the responsibility to make these judgments, nor does it render them pointless: our decisions have consequences and we are culpable for them.

I believe that these theological observations have significant import for our understanding of Scripture because, as I have just mentioned and will try to explain, the "problem of Scripture" is closely related to the "problem of evil." But before turning to Holy Scripture directly, I would suggest (for reasons that will become clear) that we briefly consider Christological matters that are relevant to our subject.

CHAPTER 3

The Contribution of Christology

The nature of Jesus Christ was a vigorously contested subject in the early church.[1] Was Jesus human, divine, or both? And if both, were the two natures "mixed" or were they somehow distinct? At the core of the debate was a widely-held philosophical belief that the divine and human natures could not be joined together in one person. One group of Christians, the *Adoptionists*, argued that Jesus was human and not divine, having become the "Son of God" because God adopted him as a son. Other Christians argued, to the contrary, that Jesus was not human at all. He was the literal and fully divine Son of God who *only appeared* to be human. This Christological view is called *Docetism*, from the Greek word *dokeō*, meaning "to appear or seem" human. Both of these views shared a belief that Jesus Christ could not have been both divine and human at the same time, and both were eventually judged heretical by Christians.

Orthodox Christianity finally affirmed that Jesus was *both* divine and human, and that the two natures did not "mix" or "blend" together but were joined in one person through a mysterious "hypostatic union." One of the Christian leaders who labored to formulate this theological viewpoint was the great church father Athanasius (c. 296-373). In his debate

---

1. For the development of Christological doctrine, see Jaroslav Pelikan, *The Christian Tradition: A History of the Development of Doctrine* (5 vols.; Chicago: University of Chicago Press, 1971-89), 1.226-77.

with the Arians, Athanasius had occasion not only to defend the divinity of Jesus but also in that context to explain those biblical texts that indicated Jesus was subject to human limitations. Two relevant texts were Luke 2:52 and Mark 13:32, which respectively said that the young Jesus "grew in wisdom and stature" and that, later on, he did not know when the end would come. "Only the Father knows," Jesus said. Athanasius argued that Jesus knew these things in his divine nature, but "as a man He is ignorant of it, for ignorance is proper to man, and especially ignorance of these things."[2] One implication of this observation (though not quite appreciated by Athanasius) is that, humanly speaking, Jesus was a finite person who grew up in Palestine, learned Hebrew and Aramaic, and was not only born Jewish but, culturally speaking, *became* Jewish.

Now it is quite true that the church fathers were not entirely consistent on these matters. In spite of their clear confession that Jesus was truly human ("of one substance with ourselves"),[3] the Fathers often argued that Jesus was never ignorant like other human beings but only feigned this as an accommodation to his human audience.[4] As Colin Gunton has pointed out, much Christian teaching over the centuries has fallen into this Docetic fault by hinting of an "unreal humanity" in Jesus.[5] I wish to avoid this Docetic tendency by siding strongly with Athanasius: Jesus, being a man, lived out his life within a finite human horizon.

At any rate, we should take note that the orthodox view of Jesus does not reflect the highest possible Christology. Rather than accepting the "high" Docetic view that Jesus was God feigning humanity, the church has elected to embrace the more complicated and mysterious belief that Jesus was fully divine and fully human at the same time. This affirmation raises an obvious question. Though Jesus was undoubtedly sinless (see Heb 4:15), did he nonetheless embrace not only our finiteness but also our fallen condition? Did Jesus Christ have a fallen human nature?

It is safe to say that, on the whole, the early Christian tradition denied

---

2. See *Against the Arians* 3.43 (NPNF2 4.417).

3. See the Definition of Chalcedon (AD 451).

4. See the patristic comments on Mark 13:32 in Thomas C. Oden and Christopher A. Hall, eds., *Mark* (ACCS; Downers Grove, IL: InterVarsity, 1998), 191-94.

5. Colin E. Gunton, *Christ and Creation* (Grand Rapids: Eerdmans, 1992), 49.

that Jesus shared in our fallen nature.[6] Gregory of Nyssa declared that Jesus was "invested with our sinful nature," but this was exceptional among the Fathers, and Gregory himself nearly repealed the claim later on in the same book.[7] Given their discomfort with considering the finiteness of Jesus, we cannot expect the fathers to help us much with this question, at least directly. But there is indirect help of great importance.

Respecting the incarnation, it was Gregory of Nazianzus who provided the classic theological argument: "what is not assumed is not redeemed."[8] His judgment was eminently logical and in keeping with Scripture's testimony that Christ "had to be made like his brethren in every respect . . . to make expiation for the sins of the people" (Heb 2:17). I cannot say whether Gregory realized it, but his argument certainly suggests that Jesus had to embrace our fallen condition in order to redeem us. Such a reading of Gregory's theology resonates well with one of Paul's passing remarks about the incarnation:

> For God has done what the law, weakened by the flesh, could not do: by sending his own Son *in the likeness of sinful flesh,* and to deal with sin, he condemned sin in the flesh, so that the just requirement of the law might be fulfilled in us, who walk not according to the flesh but according to the Spirit. (Rom 8:3-4)

As a rule, the fathers were not very comfortable with the idea that Jesus had a fallen nature, but I find it more reasonable — and more Scriptural — to affirm that Jesus was both finite and fallen, in all respects like us, "sin excepted" (Heb 4:15). This is possible because the sinful nature and sinful

6. Heen and Krey argue that "All of the Fathers were clear that Christ took on the form of sinful flesh and assumed all our weaknesses but without sin." This is true of their words, but I am not sure that by this the fathers meant that Jesus shared our fallen *nature.* If this is indeed what they intended, then the evidence sides more strongly with the theological arguments that I make here. See Erik M. Heen and Philip D. W. Krey, eds., *Hebrews* (ACCS; Downers Grove, IL: InterVarsity, 2005), 65.

7. Gregory of Nyssa, *Life of Moses* 2.32, 275, in Abraham J. Malherbe and Everett Ferguson, *Gregory of Nyssa: The Life of Moses* (New York: Paulist, 1978), 40, 116.

8. Gregory of Nazianzus, *Epistle* 101 (NPNF2 7.439-42). See discussion in Gerald O'Collins, *Christology: A Biblical, Historical, and Systematic Study of Jesus* (Oxford: Oxford University Press, 1995), 154-58.

deeds are two different things (infants may have a sinful nature, for instance, but they are not yet "sinners"). Thus the implication of ancient orthodoxy and explicit judgment of many modern theologians is that Jesus did have a fallen nature.[9] In fact, many theologians would describe this as "good news." After all, what victory did Christ win for us if fallen flesh itself were not redeemed and resurrected?

In some way or other, Jesus lived within the limits of his humanity and, it would seem, shared in our fallen nature. To what extent did this human horizon influence his teachings? I. Howard Marshall has proposed that Jesus, in his parables, assumed a doctrine of hell (as an abode of horrendous, eternal torment) that is not wholly compatible with a Christian theology of love and compassion.[10] Marshall writes:

> There would be universal agreement among civilized people that no human being should perpetrate horrors of the kind described in the parabolic imagery; those who do so are branded as war criminals and are guilty of crimes against humanity. . . . It is incredible that God should so act. So we are alerted to the conclusion that the imagery in the parables is imagery belonging to a time in the society that was accustomed to such things in real life and saw no incongruity in portraying divine judgment in this way. But we can no longer think of God in this way, even if this is imagery used by Jesus.

If Marshall is right, this would mean that Jesus, truly human as he was, expressed his theological vision using concepts that were native to his Jewish heritage.

I am sympathetic with Marshall's point. For it seems to me that "no Christology is adequate which tries either to evade the material determinateness of Jesus or his Jewish particularity."[11] In principle, the theology

9. For recent theological arguments that Jesus had a fallen nature but was not sinful, see Thomas G. Weinandy, *In the Likeness of Sinful Flesh: An Essay on the Humanity of Christ* (New York: T. & T. Clark, 2006); Ian A. McFarland, *In Adam's Fall: A Meditation on the Christian Doctrine of Original Sin* (Malden, MA: Wiley-Blackwell, 2010).

10. I. Howard Marshall, *Beyond the Bible: Moving from Scripture to Theology* (Grand Rapids: Baker, 2004), 66-69.

11. Gunton, *Christ and Creation*, 41.

of Jesus was largely the theology of a first-century Jew. And where that first-century theology was limited in its vision, so too was the theological vision of Jesus. Orthodoxy only demands that Jesus was sinless, not that his teachings were wholly insulated from the human condition.

If there are difficulties in Marshall's thesis, these involve the long-standing Christian debate about the *communicatio idiomatum* ("sharing of attributes") between Jesus' divine and human natures. To what extent were divine qualities of Jesus Christ "communicated" to his humanity? Did the insights of divine omniscience in some way inform his human perspective? And if so, did this insight prevent Jesus from using theological images from his own day that are now, by our standards, problematic? These questions quickly take us into the deepest of theological mysteries. But if we attend to the general theological, biblical, and anthropological evidence available to us, my sense is that the evidence sides strongly with Marshall's approach. Jesus did not depend on unusual divine resources to live a holy life. Rather, he lived in holiness by the same resource that animates every Christian: by the ministry of the Holy Spirit.[12]

But to return to our main theme, much to the chagrin of the Docetists and their ilk, God did not redeem us in Christ by coming "alongside" the fallen cosmos as a human-looking phantom. His redemptive work came in and through that fallen order itself, by full human participation in a world that needed healing. Docetists judged that this gospel would be too "messy," entailing as it does God's close contact with a soiled world. But orthodoxy holds that, in God's wisdom, this is precisely the point: fallen creation is redeemed only when God participates in the fallen creation. So far as we know, there was no other way to save us or our world.

Christology and Scripture: Exploring the Christological Analogy

At this point we turn from Christology to Holy Scripture. Many Christians have appealed to the "Christological analogy" to explain the nature of Scripture. They suppose that just as God brought together divinity and humanity in the incarnation, so in Scripture these two natures are joined.

---

12. See Heb 9:14; Gunton, *Christ and Creation*, 50-57.

Most theologians would admit that there is *something* useful in an exploration of this analogy, but among very conservative Christians the argument sometimes takes a particular turn and is understood as evidence for a particular view of Scripture. According to this logic, because God has given us Jesus Christ as a sinless and errorless word in the flesh, we can say by analogy that he has also given us a sinless and errorless word in Scripture.[13] Readers familiar with this strand of Christian tradition will know that it advocates the doctrine of "inerrancy," which believes that there are no *human* errors at all — not even one — in the entirety of Scripture from Genesis to Revelation. This view of Scripture is especially prevalent among conservative fundamentalists and evangelicals, though it also shows up in some other quarters of Christian theology. For the sake of convenience, I will refer to this view as *biblicism,* so called because its adherents believe that an inerrant Bible gives them foolproof access to the fundamentals of Christian doctrine and Christian living.[14] In fact, one of these fundamentals is that the Bible is inerrant in the way just described.

The first difficulty with biblicism's assertion about Christology and Scripture is that, as we have seen, though orthodoxy certainly demands that Jesus was sinless, we can by no means assume that his teachings were wholly insulated from the human condition. A good case can be made for the idea that Jesus expressed his theology using imagery (sometimes violent imagery) that was shaped and bounded by perspectives prevalent in his own day. So the Christological analogy does not necessarily support this particular view of biblical inerrancy because the biblical authors would have been limited in their perspectives, just as Jesus was. The other and more important difficulty is that, whatever Scripture is, it is *not* a hypostatic union in which divinity and humanity are mysteriously joined in one person.[15] We

13. See the "Chicago Statement on Biblical Hermeneutics," in *Hermeneutics, Inerrancy and the Bible,* ed. E. D. Radmacher and R. D. Preus (Grand Rapids: Zondervan, 1984), 881-87.

14. For a sociologically informed analysis, see the recent book by Christian Smith, *The Impossibility of Evangelical Biblicism* (Grand Rapids: Brazos Press, 2011).

15. For recent critiques of this analogy, see A. T. B. McGowan, *The Divine Authenticity of Scripture: Retrieving an Evangelical Heritage* (Downers Grove, IL: InterVarsity, 2007), 119-21; John Webster, *Holy Scripture: A Dogmatic Sketch* (Cambridge: Cambridge University Press, 2003), 22-23; Telford Work, *Living and Active: Scripture in the Economy of Salvation* (Grand Rapids: Eerdmans, 2002), 27.

certainly have this unity in the incarnation, in Jesus Christ, but in Scripture we do not have anything like this. Neither Paul, nor Luke, nor any of the other biblical authors were both divine and human. They were human beings only — good men, perhaps, but also fallible sinners in need of redemption, who wrote texts that the church has nevertheless embraced as God's word.

A *direct* analogy that moves from Christology to bibliology does not work. Rather, if we wish to draw a theological analogy from the old Christological debates that explains Scripture's character, I would suggest that the adoptionist metaphor is closer to the mark. Understood in this way, Scripture is God's word because God providentially adopted ancient human beings, like Paul, as his spokespersons. In doing so God "set apart" or "sanctified" their words for use in his redemptive activity.[16] Hence, we can affirm with a straight face that Scripture, while written by sinful human beings, is rightly referred to as *Sacred* or *Holy* Scripture. I will explore this theme in more detail below.

But again, to repeat the main and important point, the Christological analogy does not really apply directly to a doctrine of Scripture and, even if it did, it would not support but would more likely weaken arguments in support of biblicism's view of Scripture and inerrancy. We may assume, for theological and practical reasons, that the human beings who wrote Scripture erred as all humans do.

16. Webster, *Holy Scripture*, 27-30.

CHAPTER 4

The Problem of Sacred Scripture

Our theme in this chapter is the "problem" of Scripture. Does this theme necessarily imply some element of sacrilege or impiety? Is it "kosher" to interrogate God's word? These are undoubtedly among the first questions that come to a pious mind. My sense is that, if we allow Scripture to speak for itself, then the answer, at least in part, must be that it is acceptable to ask hard questions of God and Scripture. Consider, for example, the author of Psalm 89. He was well aware of God's ancient promise (see 2 Sam 7) that King David's children would never cease to reign on the throne of Israel:

Of old thou didst speak in a vision to thy faithful one, and say:
I have set the crown upon one who is mighty,
    I have exalted one chosen from the people.
I have found David, my servant;
    with my holy oil I have anointed him. . . .
My steadfast love I will keep for him forever. . . .
I will establish his line forever. . . .
If his children forsake my law . . .
I will punish their transgression . . .
    but I will not remove from him my steadfast love, or be false to my
        faithfulness.
I will not violate my covenant,

or alter the word that went forth from my lips.
Once for all I have sworn by my holiness;
   I will not lie to David.
His line shall endure forever,
   his throne as long as the sun before me.
Like the moon it shall be established for ever;
   it shall stand firm while the skies endure.

(Ps 89:19-37)

According to this promise, even acts of unfaithfulness by David's children could not jeopardize the Davidic throne. Yet this Psalmist wrote during the Exile, when the Babylonians had indeed brought David's kingdom to an abrupt end. In this disturbing situation he did not hesitate to voice his opinion that God had indeed broken his covenant with David:

But now thou hast cast off and rejected,
   thou art full of wrath against thy anointed.
Thou hast renounced the covenant with thy servant;
   thou hast defiled his crown in the dust. . . .
Thou hast removed the scepter from his hand,
   and cast his throne to the ground.

(Ps 89:38-44)

I am not interested in the immediate problem faced by the psalmist, which I will address in principle as we move forward in the discussion.[1] Rather, I wish to accentuate that here, in the Bible itself, God has canonically preserved a question about the content of his word and about his faithfulness to it. That this question was asked out of honesty and piety is reflected in the Psalm's conclusion: "Blessed be Yahweh forever. Amen, and Amen." So, while one can undoubtedly raise questions about Scrip-

---

1. Later Israelite theologians concluded from these events that the Davidic promise must have been conditional and, because of that, they added 1 Kgs 2:1-4 to the biblical text. According to this addition (and in contrast to the original promise), the conduct of David's sons *did* affect whether God would keep his promise to David. The seminal study on this matter is Frank Moore Cross, *Canaanite Myth and Hebrew Epic: Essays in the History and the Religion of Israel* (Cambridge: Harvard University Press, 1973), 274-90.

ture with impiety, it is not necessarily impious to inquire about "the problem of Scripture."

Moreover, to foreshadow where we are headed, in the end we will find that the problems in Scripture have nothing really to do with God. Like the troubles in our cosmos, the Bible's problems were caused by sinful human beings. God is in the business of resolving rather than causing these difficulties. Hence, questions about the human dimensions of Scripture need not imply contempt for God's word. We can honor God and his word even as we raise questions about the human beings who wrote Scripture.

Before I begin to outline this matter in earnest, I should point out that, in my opinion, there are potential downsides in a focused discussion of Scripture's "problems." In any inquiry into the "problems" of something, even of something otherwise very good, there is a danger that hyper-focused attention on difficulties and weaknesses will create or foster the wrong impression. If we do nothing but listen to news broadcasts about wars and weather disasters, read books on the Nazi regime, and take walks in inner-city slums, then it is inevitable that we will overlook and under-value what is truly beautiful about our world: the birth of a new child, a family enjoying a meal together, sunrises and sunsets, broad skies and green trees, and the exciting diversity of human cultures and animal life. All this beauty is easily squelched out if we morbidly focus on what is bad. The best perspective on our world is fostered though a balanced experience with what is good about it and what its problems are.

Now, respecting Scripture, the difficulty that precipitates my discussion is this: though the Bible is the word of God and, as such, is at first blush expected to be consistent in its viewpoints and, like God, free of any error, a thoughtful reading of Scripture suggests that it is neither wholly consistent nor error free. Let us consider just one clear but fairly innocuous example. Consider the two accounts of the death of Judas, the man who betrayed Jesus:

Matthew 27:3-8

When Judas, his betrayer, saw that Jesus was condemned, he repented and brought back the thirty pieces of silver to the chief priests and the elders. He said, "I have sinned by betraying innocent blood." But they said, "What is that to us? See to it yourself." Throwing down the pieces of silver in the temple, he departed; and he went and hanged himself. But the chief priests, taking the pieces of silver, said, "It is not lawful to put them into the treasury, since they are blood money." After conferring together, they used them to buy the potter's field as a place to bury foreigners. For this reason that field has been called the Field of Blood to this day.

Acts 1:18-19

Now this man [Judas] acquired a field with the reward of his wickedness; and falling headlong, he burst open in the middle and all his bowels gushed out. This became known to all the residents of Jerusalem, so that the field was called in their language Hakeldama, that is, Field of Blood.

It is easy to see the differences in the two accounts. In the first Judas dies by hanging, in the second by a violent fall; in the first Judas returns the money, in the second he keeps it; in the first the priests bought the field, in the second Judas bought it; in the first the field is named for its function as a burial plot, in the second its name commemorates Judas's death. While it is quite possible that one of these stories is right, or that both are partly right, I do not see how they can both be historically right in every respect.

The difficulty that I have just cited involves a tension *within* the Bible between two different texts. Another sort of tension appears when the biblical text does not square with things outside the Bible, as is the case when the biblical and scientific evidence do not cohere. A long-known example appears in Genesis 1, where we are told that God created a "firmament" or "expanse" in the sky to hold back the waters above it (vv. 6-8). As the great Christian exegete, John Calvin, said long ago, "it seems impossible and opposed to common sense that there are waters above the heavens."[2] Calvin admitted, nevertheless, that this is what the text says. He further concluded that this was not correct and that it probably reflected how ancient, uneducated Israelites understood the structure of the cosmos.[3] His conjecture has turned out to be right, since ancient texts and pictures discovered by modern scholars confirm that Israel's neighbors — even the advanced societies of Egypt and Mesopotamia — believed in the heavenly waters.[4]

The list of similar "tensions" and "contradictions" in Scripture is very long. To give just a few examples: Some texts depict God changing his mind and others claim that God never changes (Gen 6:6-7; Jas 1:17). Some texts describe God as having a physical body and others strongly assert that he does not have a body (Isa 6:1; Amos 9:1; John 4:24). Some texts say that Israel's forefathers knew God's name, Yahweh, and others explicitly claim that they did not know his name (Gen 28:16; Exod 6:2-3). One text says that God's people should boil the Passover meal and another forbids boiling it (Deut 16:7; Exod 12:9).[5] Some texts permitted Israel to sacrifice at many places before Solomon's temple was built while others did not permit this (Deut 12:8-14; Lev 17:8-9). There are texts that promise judgment

2. John Calvin, *Commentaries on the First Book of Moses, called Genesis*, tr. John King (2 vols.; Edinburgh: Calvin Translation Society, 1847-50), 1.79-80. Calvin goes on to criticize others who in spite of the obvious facts accept the heavenly waters "by faith." Here Calvin probably had in his crosshairs Luther, who said something like this in his Lectures on Genesis (*Luther's Works* 1, ed. J. Pelikan [St. Louis, MO: Concordia Publishing, 1958], 30, 42, 43). Nonetheless, Calvin was not always sympathetic with science, taking his stand, for instance, against Copernican cosmology in a sermon on 1 Corinthians (Calvin's sermon no. 8 on 1 Corinthians, cited in W. J. Bouwsma, *John Calvin: A Sixteenth Century Portrait* [Oxford: University Press, 1988], 72).

3. In his own words, "Moses wrote everywhere in homely style.... Certainly in the first chapter [of Genesis] he did not treat scientifically the stars, as a philosopher would; but he called them in a popular manner, according to their appearance to the uneducated *rather than according to truth*" (italics added). See *Commentaries on the First Book of Moses, called Genesis*, 1.256-57.

4. See Kenton L. Sparks, *Ancient Texts for the Study of the Hebrew Bible: A Guide to the Background Literature* (Peabody, MA: Hendrickson, 2005), 321, 325, 337.

5. Note that some translations (such as the NIV) attempt to "fix" this problem by translating the two texts in a compatible way. But the Hebrew text of Deuteronomy clearly says that the Israelites should boil the Passover, and with equal clarity Exodus commands that they should roast it and should not boil it.

on the children of sinners, and those that say God certainly does not harm children for the sins of their parents (Exod 20:5; Deut 24:16).[6] Some texts aver that God's people should divorce unbelieving spouses, and others say that we certainly should not divorce them (Ezra 9–10; 1 Cor 7:10-16). We have a text that says Jesus' family was originally from Nazareth, and another that says they were from Bethlehem (Luke 2:1-4; Matthew 1–2); in a related matter, we have a text that says Jesus moved to Nazareth soon after his birth and also a text that says this happened several years later (Luke 2:39-40; Matthew 1–2). We have a text that says that idol worshippers are without excuse, but another that excuses them (Rom 1:18-23; Acts 17:29-31). One text says that David was an adulterer and murderer, and another portrays him as wholly righteous and innocent (2 Samuel 11–12; 1 Chronicles). One text says King David paid 50 shekels of silver for Israel's temple site, and another that he paid 600 shekels *of gold* (2 Sam 24:24; 1 Chron 21:25). We have a text that says the world will inevitably hate Christians, and another that encourages Christians to pursue peace with all people (John 15:18-21; Heb 12:14). We have a text that claims God is not willing for anyone to perish, and another that seems to say he predestines some human beings to eternal judgment (2 Pet 3:9; Rom 9:1-24). On the scientific front, the Bible ostensibly indicates the earth is a few thousand years old, yet science tells us that it is billions of years old. The Bible says human beings were created on day 6 of a six-day creation process, and science that tells us human beings were created through a complex evolutionary process that took millions of years. The Bible claims that there was a worldwide flood that killed almost every living thing, and geological and biological evidence proves that this never happened.

The problem of Scripture's diversity is not limited to these discrete cases but arises as well respecting the biblical canon as a whole. The church required several centuries for its list of New Testament books to take on a final, definitive form, and it has never reached full agreement on what books constitute the Old Testament.[7] The problem is further exacer-

6. For related texts, see Exod 34:7; Josh 7:1-26; Jer 31:29-30; and especially Ezek 18:1-29.

7. Catholics and Orthodox embrace somewhat different versions of the Apocrypha, while Protestants generally reject it. As a result, Karl Barth has commented that "the Church can and must [in fact always does] continually ask concerning the legitimacy of the traditional Canon." See Barth, *Church Dogmatics* (Edinburgh: T. & T. Clark, 1936-77), 1/2.478.

bated when we recall that early Christians included the book of Hebrews in the New Testament because they thought Paul wrote it — something few would believe anymore — and when we notice that the biblical authors sometimes treated as canonical books that were ultimately judged to be non-canonical. I have in mind the way that Jude quotes as inspired Scripture the pseudepigraphic books of 1 *Enoch* and the *Assumption of Moses* (Jude 9, 14).[8]

In some cases the apparent contradictions and problems that I have just outlined can perhaps be "harmonized" in some way or other. For instance, some scholars have suggested that one of the conflicting accounts of Judas's death (the account in Matthew) was written according to the fictional conventions of Jewish "midrash" rather than the conventions of biography or history.[9] If this is right, then there is no *historical* conflict between the two biblical stories of Judas's death. But it is very doubtful — in fact, I would say impossible — that all these problems and countless others that I have not mentioned would have workable, convincing solutions. If we take the Bible's explicit content with any seriousness, then it is as clear as it can possibly be that its authors were not wholly consistent with each other, nor were they wholly right about all matters of science and history. Like any other book, the Bible appears to be a historically and culturally contingent text and, because of that, it reflects the diverse viewpoints of different people who lived in different times and places. Dietrich Bonhoeffer put it this way:

> The Bible remains a book like other books. One must be ready to accept the concealment within history and therefore let historical criticism run its course. But it is through the Bible, with all its flaws, that the risen one encounters us. We must get into the troubled waters of historical criticism. Its importance is not absolute, but neither is it unimportant. Certainly it will not lead to a weakening, but rather to a strengthening

8. As Augustine said, "We cannot deny that Enoch, the seventh from Adam, left some divine writings, for this is asserted by the Apostle Jude in his canonical epistle." See *City of God* 15.23 (NPNF1 2.305).

9. Michael D. Goulder, *Midrash and Lection in Matthew* (London: SPCK, 1974); Robert Gundry, *Matthew: A Commentary on His Literary and Theological Art* (Grand Rapids: Eerdmans, 1982).

of faith, because the concealment within the historical belongs to the humiliation of Christ.[10]

In other words, the Bible *is* human tradition, written by authors of whom "not only part but all that they say is historically related and conditioned."[11]

For some Christians, the foregoing observations will suggest that the Bible, as the word of God, is far too human. Yet the problems just cited are not, in my view, the most serious difficulties that Christians face in the Bible. More troublesome are those cases where a biblical text espouses ethical values that not only contradict other biblical texts but strike us as truly sinister and evil. Consider the contrast between Matthew and Deuteronomy:

Matthew 5:43-45	**Deuteronomy 20:16-18**
You have heard that it was said, "You shall love your neighbor and hate your enemy." But I say to you, Love your enemies and pray for those who persecute you, so that you may be children of your Father in heaven; for he makes his sun rise on the evil and on the good, and sends rain on the righteous and on the unrighteous.	But as for the towns of these peoples that Yahweh your God is giving you as an inheritance, you must not let anything that breathes remain alive. You shall annihilate them — the Hittites and the Amorites, the Canaanites and the Perizzites, the Hivites and the Jebusites — just as Yahweh your God has commanded, so that they may not teach you to do all the abhorrent things that they do for their gods, and you thus sin against Yahweh your God.

These words from the lips of Jesus and the Law of Moses are profoundly different. How can one biblical text admonish us to love our enemies and

---

10. Dietrich Bonhoeffer, *Christ the Center*, tr. E. H. Robertson (London: Harper, 1978), 74.

11. Barth, *Church Dogmatics*, 1/2.509. For a Catholic argument that the Bible is "nothing other than tradition," see Cardinal Joseph Ratzinger and Vittorio Messori, *The Ratzinger Report: An Exclusive Interview on the State of the Church*, tr. S. Attanasio and G. Harrison (San Francisco: Ignatius, 1985), 160.

another command Israel to commit genocide against ethnic groups because they have a different religion?

The problem and its scope are suggested, I think, by the Bible's account of the destruction of the Canaanite city of Jericho:

> So the people [of Israel] shouted, and the trumpets were blown. As soon as the people heard the sound of the trumpets, they raised a great shout, and the wall fell down flat; so the people charged straight ahead into the city and captured it. Then they "devoted to destruction" (ḥerem) by the edge of the sword all in the city, both men and women, young and old, oxen, sheep, and donkeys. (Josh 6:20-21)

Here Israel is rewarded by success because, in the book of Joshua, righteousness amounted to obediently exterminating Canaanite men, women, children, and animals. In fact, in the theology of Deuteronomy and Joshua, this was an act of ḥerem, a ritual of complete devotion that sacrificed the Canaanites and their belongings to God.[12] In carrying out this ritual act, Deuteronomy specifically commanded the Israelites to resist the natural tendency to "show mercy" to their human enemies; compassion was to be avoided at all cost (see Deut 7:2).

If we are troubled by these texts — and I think that if we are really honest, we should be — then we will be still more troubled when we recall that, for generations, Jewish and Christian readers of the Bible have used these texts to justify wholesale, violent, exterminations of their enemies.

Though in broad strokes we might describe the problem of Scripture as its "diversity," on closer inspection I think that the problem actually falls into three interrelated types of issues: (1) the problem of human finiteness, (2) the problem of culture, and (3) the problem of human fallenness. As I will try to explain below, it is only this last and most serious problem — the problem of human fallenness — that is closely related to the "problem of evil" that confronts us so palpably in the created order. Let us consider each problem in turn.

First we have the problem of human finiteness. For instance, when

---

12. See Norbert Lohfink, "חרם ḥāram," in *Theological Dictionary of the Old Testament*, vol. 5, ed. G. J. Botterweck and H. Ringgren (Grand Rapids: Eerdmans, 1974), 180-99.

Genesis tells us that there are "waters above the heavens," it does so from a finite human perspective that really believed there were such waters. Surely this view was wrong, as John Calvin long ago pointed out, but *that* it is wrong is neither a surprise nor particularly consequential. It is not so different from the natural but erroneous belief that the earth is flat. From the New Testament we have this example of humanity's finite perspective: While Luke tells us that the apostle Paul went to Damascus and then to Jerusalem to meet the disciples immediately after his conversion, Paul's explicit personal testimony is that he certainly *did not* go to Damascus or Jerusalem but proceeded instead to Arabia for a long period of spiritual retreat (Acts 9; Gal 1:15-20). Assuming that Paul is telling us the truth (he actually says, "I am not lying"), it would seem that Luke had some of his facts wrong. Luke's error is no more surprising than the errant cosmology of Genesis, for in both cases we are reading the words of fallible authors who in turn depended on sources and traditions that were produced by fallible people. Human beings err, and this accounts in part for the errant and diverse perspectives that sometimes appear in Scripture. So there is no need to "harmonize" the Bible with modern science or to make Paul and Luke agree in all respects.

A second kind of problem in Scripture arises because of variations in culture. When one biblical text demands that the Passover sacrifice be "roasted" while another demands "boiling" (Exod 12:9; Deut 16:7), this difference is not deeply metaphysical but merely reflects diverse social conditions that produced different views of acceptable ritual practice. The diversity stems from a cultural gap that separated one biblical author from another. In terms of theological significance, the difference between the Passover regulations finally amounts to something like the difference between the eighteenth amendment of the U.S. Constitution, which forbade the consumption of alcohol, and the twenty-first amendment that permitted it. These two legal statutes certainly contradict each other, but neither is finally "right" and, ultimately, either might be a wise and acceptable practice given historical and social conditions.

A variation of this cultural gap opens up between the biblical writers and later readers such as ourselves. To give an example, when we read that biblical law required a rapist to marry his victim without the possibility of divorce (Deut 22:28-29), we are understandably repulsed by what looks like very sick and twisted logic. But the law actually served a role in defending the woman's rights.[13] Because ancient Israelites greatly valued virginity, rape victims tended to remain unmarried and, hence, to become economically vulnerable in a patriarchal world. Given this eventuality, rapists were forced to marry and economically care for their victims. This biblical legislation closely paralleled practices elsewhere in the ancient world and not only protected the woman after the rape but also tended to forestall rape by forcing would-be rapists to consider the potentially dire, lifelong consequences of their actions.[14] So, though I freely admit that I am troubled by the law as it stands, the law is "good" in ways I would not have expected because my world is so profoundly different from the world of ancient Israel.

The third problem in Scripture is the most serious because it touches on the very heart of the gospel message. I refer, again, to the Bible's ethical and moral diversity, to the fact that Jesus summed up the law and Gospel in the words, "Love God and love your neighbor," and that this summation of Scripture — with its concomitant responsibility to love our enemies, to turn the other cheek, and to pray for those who persecute us — stands in glaring contrast to texts that list women as property, that praise God for smashing infants against rocks, that allow slave owners to beat their slaves, and that present God as commanding the extermination of ethnic and religious groups.[15] It is this particular problem, and the questions raised by it, that brings us back to the problem of evil that confronts us so transparently in the created order — to the problems of genocide, rape, murder, abuse, oppression, war, famine, disease, and suffering, as well as to the more subtle but undeniably painful experiences of personal isolation, disappointment, and depression that strike so many who live in the "safest" and "healthiest" quarters of modern society.

There is a tendency among more conservative Christians to imagine that the ethical problem referred to here is really an illusion created by

13. See Jeffrey Tigay, *Deuteronomy* (Philadelphia; Jerusalem: Jewish Publication Society, 1996), 208-9.

14. See MAL A, §55 in Martha T. Roth, *Law Collections from Mesopotamia and Asia Minor* (2nd ed., SBLWAW 6; Atlanta: Scholars, 1997), 174-75.

15. The relevant texts (respectively) are Exod 20:17; Ps 137:9; Exod 21:20-21; Deuteronomy 7.

misplaced modern sensibilities, that this is just another case in which "contemporary human ethics" arrogantly presume to be better than "God's biblical ethics."[16] While I do not doubt that modern ethics run amok in many ways and means, I do not think that this objection carries much weight.

Anyone familiar with the history of Christian theology will know how much early Christians struggled with the Bible's ethical diversity. Consider these comments from the pen of the great Cappadocian Father, Gregory of Nyssa (c. 335-395), who was deeply troubled by God's execution of Egyptian children in the Passover story of Exodus:

> The Egyptian [Pharaoh] acts unjustly, and in his place is punished his newborn child, who in his infancy cannot discern what is good and what is not. . . . If such a one now pays the penalty of his father's evil, where is justice? Where is piety? Where is holiness? Where is Ezekiel, who cries . . . "The son should not suffer for the sin of the father"? How can history so contradict reason?

Gregory concluded that, ethically speaking, the Passover story simply could not pass as literal history: it is an allegory about sin that directs us to destroy evil quickly before it grows too troublesome for us.[17] Now my point is not whether Gregory handled the difficulty as we would, for it seems very doubtful to me, and perhaps to most modern readers, that the author of Exodus intended an allegory. But Gregory's method aside, his fourth-century comment shows that the ethical problems in Scripture are *not* the result of modern imagination run amok. This judgment is reinforced by many other instances in which the church fathers either ignored problem texts or read them as allegories.[18] In fact, if we carefully consider the most profound differences between the Old and New Testaments, we

---

16. For a short catalogue of conservative interpretive strategies, see Eric A. Seibert, *Disturbing Divine Behavior: Troubling Old Testament Images of God* (Minneapolis: Fortress, 2009), 69-88.

17. Gregory of Nyssa, *Life of Moses* 2.91-93 in Abraham J. Malherbe and Everett Ferguson, *Gregory of Nyssa: The Life of Moses* (New York: Paulist, 1978), 75-76.

18. For a survey of early Christian allegories on the Deuteronomic genocide, see Douglas S. Earl, "The Christian Significance of Deuteronomy 7," *JTI* 3 (2009): 41-62.

will notice soon enough that the biblical authors themselves were uncomfortable with the violent streak in some biblical (mostly Old Testament) texts. This leads to my next point.

I suspect that we cannot too quickly assume that "modern ethics" can be pitted against biblical values. One could argue, at least in part, that the modern, liberal, democratic critique of violence, genocide, and ethnic oppression was engendered by Scripture, especially in liberal theological traditions that seized on the softer, more compassionate side of Scripture.[19] If this is right, then we have before us the fascinating paradox that modern resistance to biblical violence actually originated in the Bible itself.

Regardless, my main point is that the ethical problems I speak of are very obvious to thoughtful readers of Scripture in any era of church history. This is because the problems are not the inventions of arrogant human readers who stand in judgment over Scripture. Rather, the problems are engendered by the fact that Scripture sometimes renders judgment on itself.

In chapter 1, we noted that people respond to the problem of evil in different ways. The same can be said of Scripture's ethical problem. Some have concluded that, because of these difficulties, Scripture simply cannot be the word of God.[20] As Franz Buggle expressed it, "This is what the psalms really are: in large part, and to a degree seldom encountered otherwise, a text dominated by primitive and uncontrolled feelings of hatred, desire for vengeance, and self-righteousness. . . . [F]or a long time, I have not read any text so marked by excessive and unbridled hatred and thirst for revenge."[21] Just as the serious problems in the cosmos are thought by some to preclude belief in a good God and good creation, so the serious problems in Scripture are taken to preclude its identity as the good word

19. Regarding the influence of Christian and biblical ideas on Western notions of justice and rights, see Nicholas Wolterstorff, *Justice: Rights and Wrongs* (Princeton: Princeton University Press, 2008).

20. Bart D. Ehrman, *God's Problem: How the Bible Fails to Answer Our Most Important Question — Why We Suffer* (New York: HarperOne, 2008); Hector Avalos, *Fighting Words: The Origins of Religious Violence* (Amherst, NY: Prometheus, 2005); F. Buggle, *Denn sie wissen nicht, was sie glauben, oder warum man redlicherweise nicht mehr Christ sein kann. Eine Streitschrift* (Reinbek: Rowohlt, 1992).

21. Buggle, *Denn sie wissen nicht*, 79-80.

of a good God. "If a good God truly existed," they say, "and if Scripture were truly his word, then Scripture would present a consistent and beautiful ethical vision, wholly consistent in matters of love and morality." But this does not appear to be what Scripture offers. So Scripture is not the word of God. This is the logic.

Another approach to the problem, common among very conservative Christians, is what I have described as fundamentalist biblicism. Its approach to Scripture's problems is roughly akin, in my opinion, to how Christian Science handles the problem of evil. In spite of the very obvious evidence otherwise, Christian Science holds that the "evil" in our world is really an illusion, that the world actually *is* wholly good, and that we should embrace and be healed by that belief. In a similar way, fundamentalism holds that Scripture's apparent diversity — its internal inconsistencies, its tensions with historical and scientific evidence, and its supposed ethical diversity — is actually an illusion created by careless interpretation or by malevolent scholarly efforts to undermine the Bible's authority. So the Bible presents us not with real problems but with "apparent problems" invented by skeptics.[22] Hence, when it comes to Israel's massacre of the Canaanites, fundamentalists will argue that the carnage was just fine and probably not as bad as it sounds.[23]

While I quite agree that there are religious skeptics who harbor malevolence towards the Christian faith and who for this reason work to give the Bible a bad name, I do not believe that the whole problem of Scripture can be blamed on the skeptics; still less can we embrace the Canaanite genocide as a wholesome portrait of moral action.

Some forward-thinking conservative scholars have tried to resolve the difficulties by appeals to "speech act" or genre theory.[24] These scholars

22. For an example of this approach, see Gleason L. Archer, *Encyclopedia of Bible Difficulties* (Grand Rapids: Zondervan, 1982).

23. For recent "not as bad as it sounds" arguments, see Paul Copan, *Is God a Moral Monster? Making Sense of the Old Testament God* (Grand Rapids: Baker, 2011); David T. Lamb, *God Behaving Badly: Is the God of the Old Testament Angry, Sexist and Racist?* (Downers Grove: InterVarsity, 2011).

24. Kevin J. Vanhoozer, *The Drama of Doctrine: A Canonical-Linguistic Approach to Christian Theology* (Louisville: Westminster John Knox Press, 2005); Timothy Ward, *Words of Life: Scripture as the Living and Active Word of God* (Downers Grove: InterVarsity, 2009).

are savvy enough to notice that Scripture appears to get things wrong, but in these cases they argue that Scripture's true substance is not really about whatever appears to be in error. So, for example, when Joshua demands the slaughter of Canaanites, these scholars will aver that the biblical author's "speech act" — the thing the author sought to accomplish in Joshua — had nothing to do with warfare but rather was an attempt to "construct Israelite identity."[25] Hence Joshua is better understood as a "myth" that uses the conquest story to teach good theology.

As appealing as this approach is, it seems to me that, in the end, it fails to resolve the difficulties. For whether they did so through myth or history, the authors of Deuteronomy and Joshua certainly did portray genocide as spiritually laudable behavior. The simple fact is that "the devil does not have to work very hard to find biblical precedents for the legitimation of violence."[26] The ethical problems in Scripture are real.

I take it that many Christian readers, both liberal and conservative, will find themselves somewhere between the extremes represented by fundamentalism and skepticism. They embrace the Bible as God's word but are somewhat troubled by the difficulties in Scripture, most especially by the ethical problems to which I have just referred. In the pages that follow I will try to suggest a way forward that engages Scripture as God's word while admitting, at the same time, that the ethical diversity that it displays is a factual problem. My proposal closely follows the contours of traditional Christian responses to the problem of evil.

I should mention, before moving on, that I do not construe this book as a book about Scripture's *ethical* problems. Rather, I emphasize the ethical difficulties on the assumption that these are the most important problems we face in Scripture. If we acquire robust strategies for engaging the Bible's ethical diversity, then presumably we will be better positioned to address Scripture's diversity on less pressing matters, such as science, history, and theology.

---

25. As an example, see the recent monograph by Douglas S. Earl, *The Joshua Delusion? Rethinking Genocide in the Bible* (Eugene, OR: Cascade, 2010).

26. John J. Collins, "The Zeal of Phinehas: The Bible and the Legitimation of Violence," *JBL* 122 (2003): 3-21.

CHAPTER 5

The Brokenness of Scripture

When someone in Western culture wishes to emphasize how bad things have been or are in our world, one turns almost invariably to the era of the Second World War and the *Shoah* (or "Holocaust") as an example. The Shoah fascinates our Western imagination because it was perpetrated against the Jews by a very educated, modern, sophisticated, highly industrial German society that stood directly within our own Judeo-Christian tradition. That it was possible for the horrific events to unfold under those modern conditions stands as a perpetual and important reminder that we are never so educated, advanced, or "enlightened" that we cannot fall into the trap of hating and killing innocent people. The Shoah has become *the* quintessential symbol of our fallen world and of fallen, sinful humanity.

But is it not a very deep paradox that the Shoah, in which Nazis systematically exterminated the Jews because of their religion and ethnicity, is mirrored so vividly by the Deuteronomic ban in Jewish Scripture, according to which Israel exterminated the Canaanites because of their religion? And is it not troubling that this biblical command and the apparent obedience to it in Joshua stand at the very fountainhead of Israel's history, as both the proper conclusion of its origin story (in the Pentateuch) and the proper beginning of its long history in the land of Canaan? Even if we can put our finger on *some* differences between the two situations, are they not so close that any serious reader of Scripture will feel queasy thinking about it?

I am reminded, here, of a famous study by the Israeli scholar Georges Tamarin.[1] Tamarin surveyed two groups of Israeli children about the morality of genocidal conquest. To one group he told the story of Joshua's conquest of Jericho, and to the other he told the same story but substituted a Chinese general in Joshua's place. About 60% of the Israeli children approved of Joshua's conquest, but only 7% approved of the Chinese assault. One can read Tamarin's discussion for the details. His main point is also mine: the Canaanite conquest would strike us as flagrant evil were it not a story from the Bible.

What we face, I think, is the ethical difficulty I mentioned earlier in passing: the problem of scripture *is* the problem of evil. Just as God's good and beautiful creation stands in need of redemption, so Scripture — as God's word written within and in relation to that creation, by finite and fallen humans — stands in need of redemption. Scripture does more than witness explicitly to the fallenness of the created order and humanity. Scripture is implicitly, in itself, a product of and evidence for the fallen world that it describes. This is why there are texts in Scripture that strike any thoughtful observer as vile and morally compromised — texts that we simply wish were not in the Bible. The impulse to set aside these so-called "texts of terror" is so strong that the Catholic Church's *Liturgy of Hours* actually eliminates three psalms (58, 83, and 109) and omits verses from others because they are "harsh in tone" and would present difficulties in public worship.[2]

Given what we have said so far, I would join other scholars in suggesting that a robust doctrine of Scripture should not presume that "the text is immune from criticism."[3] Scripture was written by godly but fallen hu-

1. Georges R. Tamarin, *The Israeli Dilemma: Essays on a Warfare State* (Rotterdam: University Press, 1973), 183-90.

2. William L. Holladay, *The Psalms Through Three Thousand Years: Prayerbook of a Cloud of Witnesses* (Minneapolis: Fortress Press, 1993), 304-5.

3. My phrase "immune from criticism" is taken from Francis Watson, *Text, Church and World: Biblical Interpretation in Theological Perspective* (Grand Rapids: Eerdmans, 1994), 173-87, 231. For similar sentiments, see Ellen F. Davis, "Critical Traditioning: Seeking an Inner Biblical Hermeneutic," in *The Art of Reading Scripture*, ed. E. F. Davis and R. B. Hays (Grand Rapids: Eerdmans, 2003), 163-80; Werner Jeanrond, *Theological Hermeneutics: Development and Significance* (London: SCM Press, 1994), 114-15; I. Howard Marshall, *Beyond the Bible: Moving from*

man authors who sometimes thought and wrote ungodly things. If this is right, then the church should not defend Scripture's uniqueness as the divine word by appealing to its perfection. Rather, a proper account of Scripture's goodness and divine origins will closely follow the traditional Christian response to the problem of evil.

To make my point clearer, I would offer here the following parallel propositions:

> God's creation, which is good, nevertheless includes evil. But these flaws in creation should not be blamed on God but rather on humanity and its sinful, fallen state.

> God's written word, which is good, nevertheless includes evil. But these flaws in Scripture should not be blamed on God but rather on humanity and its sinful, fallen state.

Both humanity and Scripture are God's good works and serve a role in his redemptive work. And though this is true, both are marred by the effects of the Fall. The presence in Scripture of this distortion no more compromises its status as God's word than the distortion in humanity compromises its status as God's creation.

The Fall's effect on humanity and Scripture reminds us that both stand in need of redemption. In each case, we must render thoughtful judgments about where they are rightly ordered and where they reflect the Fall's disordering effects. When we make these judgments about Scripture, we follow the admonition of Augustine, who long ago taught that

> Anything in the divine writings that cannot be referred either to good, honest morals, or to the truth of the faith, you must know is said allegorically. . . . Those things . . . which appear to the inexperienced to be sinful, and which are ascribed to God, or to men whose holiness is put before us

Scripture to Theology (Grand Rapids: Baker, 2004); Eric A. Seibert, *Disturbing Divine Behavior: Troubling Old Testament Images of God* (Minneapolis: Fortress, 2009); Miroslav Volf, *Captive to the Word of God: Engaging the Scriptures for Contemporary Theological Reflection* (Grand Rapids: Eerdmans, 2010), 35. Perhaps, too, Walther Moberly, "What Is Theological Interpretation of Scripture?" *JTI* 3 (2009): 161-78.

as an example, are wholly allegorical, and the hidden kernel of meaning they contain is to be picked out as food for the nourishment of charity.[4]

While I do not fully agree with Augustine's allegorical solution, I very much agree with his sense of the problem. Scripture's natural meaning sometimes runs contrary to the Gospel and, where it does, begs for a hermeneutical explanation. Unlike Augustine, I would attribute these theological tensions to the fact that the Bible is both sacred and broken, which reflects God's choice to sanctify the broken, human voices of Scripture as his divine word.[5]

Two biblical texts attest to the awkward relationship that can surface between God's redemptive activity and the activities of sinful, fallen humanity. From the Old Testament we have the story of Joseph, in which God advanced his redemptive work through the evil deeds of Joseph's brothers, who sold Joseph into slavery. As Joseph expressed it, "though you, my brothers, intended to do harm to me, God intended it for good, in order to save numerous people, as he is doing today."[6] Paul offers a similar comment in the New Testament. When he was confronted by evangelists with questionable motives, the apostle responded: "Some indeed preach Christ from envy and rivalry, but others from good will . . . but what does it matter? . . . Christ is proclaimed in every way, whether out of false motives or true; and in that I rejoice" (Phil 1:15-18).

These texts witness succinctly to the subtle relationship between human and divine agency. Acts of human sin, intended by ill will, are understood as standing within God's providential, redemptive activity.[7] And in

---

4. *On Christian Doctrine*, 3.10, 12 (*NPNF*1 2.560-62).

5. By saying Scripture is "broken," I do not mean to suggest that it "does not work" or "cannot serve its purpose." Rather, I mean that Scripture, like everything created by God but touched by the Fall, is at the same time both beautiful *and* in need of repair. Nothing claimed here is in tension with "Scripture cannot be broken" (John 10:35). John's words are not a denial of sin's effect on Scripture. Rather, they merely restate the Jewish assumption that Scripture "always remains in force." See Barnabas Lindars, *The Gospel of John* (NCBC; Grand Rapids: Eerdmans, 1972), 374.

6. Paraphrase of Gen 50:20, adapted from the NRSV.

7. About this, see John Calvin's comments in *Institutes of the Christian Religion* 4.20.30-31 (2 vols.; London: J. Clarke, 1949, 2.674). For a masterful discussion of "providence" in the Joseph Story, see Uriel Simon, *Seek Peace and Pursue It: Topical Issues in the Light of the Bible and the Bible in the Light of Topical Issues* (Tel Aviv: Yediot Ahronot, 2002 [Hebrew]), 58-85.

spite of this — here I simply assert a dogmatic theological point — we cannot trace the human evil back to God. Humanity is ultimately responsible for what ails the world. I believe that the same conception of human and divine agency holds for Scripture. It is a book where God infallibly achieves his redemptive aims through the fallible words of human authors. Bonhoeffer put it this way: "We must read this book of books with all human methods. But through the fragile and broken Bible, God meets us in the voice of the Risen One."[8]

Admittedly, this is more of a theological *description* of the situation than a full-blown *explanation* that resolves all our questions. But I would say we can no more offer a full-orbed, detailed explanation and solution for the ethical problems in Scripture than we can offer a thorough and sensible explanation for the Nazi physicians who tortured Jewish children. We simply must confess that we do not have a complete answer. But Christians believe and affirm that the fallenness in creation, which has also influenced Scripture, is best explained by the existence of a good and righteous God who loves human beings and against whom humanity stands in rebellion. As a result, we have the paradoxical circumstance in which God's creation and written word, though truly *his,* include horrible things that he neither created nor said. These terrors, whether of life experience or biblical "texts of terror," cannot be fully resolved by really smart human beings with well-honed hermeneutical tools. They will only be resolved by the eschaton — by God's redemptive activity to set his world aright through Christ.

Though I admit there are mysteries here, genuine limitations in our understanding of Scripture and its attendant problems, it seems to me that we can explore these matters in greater detail. As we move ahead, I will try to explain how we can read Scripture as an authoritative text even when its contents are untidy, diverse, and influenced by the fallen human condition. At this point I will simply say that, among other things, any workable solution will require some manner of ordering the Bible's diversity, so that we give priority to biblical texts that speak with more clarity and deeper theological logic than those that are more partial or distorted by the human condition.

8. Dietrich Bonhoeffer, *Reflections on the Bible: Human Word and Word of God,* tr. M. E. Boring (Peabody, MA: Hendrickson, 2004), 15.

CHAPTER 6

Some Theological Queries

To what extent does my approach to the problem of Scripture stand within the Christian tradition? Is it a modern innovation, or is it related closely to things that earlier Christians have thought and said? I freely admit that, so far as I know, there are no pre-modern Christians who have explicitly suggested that the problems in Scripture closely parallel the problem of evil as it relates to the created order. I simply do not know what Augustine, Aquinas, Luther, and Calvin would say about my proposals if they lived in our own day. On the other hand, Luther openly criticized the New Testament book of James as an "epistle of straw," and Calvin was willing to admit that parts of the creation story in Genesis are scientifically wrong. So again, though I do not know what they would say, I suspect that their critical intellectual temperaments would eventually warm to my proposals. After all, men like Luther and Calvin were *very* radical figures in their own day. Anything that I am proposing is trivial when compared to their rabid criticisms of and drastic break with long-standing Catholic tradition. But these speculations and musings aside, I can say quite confidently that my proposals are closely related to the theological insights of the Christian tradition.

Foremost, the Christian tradition has long admitted that Scripture presents us with problems or apparent problems that have to be worked out. Scripture is not clean and simple. The long-standing popularity of allegorical interpretation, judiciously used to resolve Scripture's apparent contradictions by appealing to genre, is tacit evidence of this reality. As Gregory the Great once said, "Undoubtedly the words of the literal text, when they do not agree with each other, show that something else is to be sought in them."[1] Similarly, Wesley suggested that "if the literal sense of these Scriptures is absurd, and apparently contrary to reason, then we should be obliged not to interpret them according to the letter, but to look out for a looser meaning."[2] These flexible interpretive strategies — and others cited in the previous chapter — are a "smoking gun" that hints at the real challenges presented by Scripture. As we will see, the Christian tradition has on some occasions even admitted that Scripture really does say things that are not quite right.

The early fathers of the church were troubled by numerous biblical texts, but they were particularly troubled by obvious and significant differences between the Old and New Testament views of God, theology, and religious practice. Why, they asked, would God allow animal sacrifices in the Old Testament if these were pagan rites rendered superfluous by the New Testament? Here is the answer given by Gregory of Nazianzus, which I quote at length:

> And therefore like a Tutor or Physician [God] partly removes and partly condones ancestral habits, conceding some little of what tended to pleasure, just as medical men do with their patients, that their medicine may be taken, being artfully blended with what is nice. . . . For instance, in the first [dispensation] he cut off the idol, but left the sacrifices; the second, while it destroyed sacrifices did not forbid circumcision. Then, when once men had submitted to the curtailment, they also yielded that which had been conceded to them: in the first instance the sacrifices, in the second circumcision, and became instead of Gentiles, Jews, and instead of Jews, Christians, being beguiled into the Gospel by gradual changes.[3]

---

1. Gregory the Great, "Moralia in Job," in William Yarchin, *History of Biblical Interpretation* (Peabody, MA: Hendrickson, 2004), 89.

2. John Wesley, *The Works of John Wesley* (12 vols.; London: Wesleyan Methodist Book Room, 1872), 4:337.

3. Gregory of Nazianzus, *Orations* 5.25 (NPNF2 7.325-26).

Like some other Christian fathers, Gregory believed that God consented to inferior and errant practices in Scripture because humanity was not prepared to manage their sudden elimination. Gregory only hints but does not explicitly say that the eliminated practices were actually evil, but Justin did not hesitate to say it:

> We also would observe the fleshly circumcision, and the Sabbaths, and in short all of your festivals, if we did not know why they were ordained, namely, because of your sins and hardness of your hearts. . . . God enjoined you to keep the Sabbath and imposed on you other precepts for a sign, as I have already said, on account of your unrighteousness and that of your fathers.

Justin found confirmation of his view in Ezekiel's prophecy that God gave the Jews "laws that were not good."[4] That is, Justin was willing to say (following Ezekiel) that God gave his people laws that were not good precisely because his people had fallen, hardened hearts. Taken together, Gregory and Justin can easily be understood as saying: Scripture's discourse is adapted to and reflects human sinfulness, and these fallen elements of biblical religion were gradually eliminated during the redemptive process. This is very close to my own understanding of Scripture and dovetails nicely with the teaching of Jesus in Matthew 19, where he describes the Old Testament's divorce law as an accommodation to humanity's fallen condition.

Moving historically forward, I have mentioned already Calvin's view that the Genesis cosmology was errant, a view also shared by John Wesley. Wesley further admitted the possibility that the genealogies of Jesus in Luke and Matthew were contradictory because the biblical authors consulted errant Jewish genealogies.[5] So, though Calvin and Wesley were not always transparent in saying so, they recognized that the Bible could sometimes have its facts wrong.

If these "giants" of church history were willing to admit that errant

---

4. Ezek 20:25. For Justin's comments, see *Dialogue with Trypho* 18.21 (ANF 1.203-4).

5. Scott J. Jones, *John Wesley's Conception and Use of Scripture* (Nashville: Abingdon, 1995), 39-40, 79-80, 147-48.

and even sinful viewpoints were included in Scripture, how did they avoid the conclusion that God had erred in Scripture? In every case, they argued that the errors were not God's errors but rather his wise "accommodations" or "condescensions" to the spiritual and/or intellectual limitations of human beings.[6] God included the pagan sacrifices in Leviticus because Israel was hard-hearted (so Justin) and an ancient cosmology in Genesis as a concession to Israel's primitive scientific knowledge (so Calvin and Wesley). Paradoxically, these Christian scholars were able to admit the human error in Scripture and, at the same time, to affirm that God does not err in Scripture. In their theological hands, biblical error became God's wise accommodation to the intellectual and spiritual limitations of the human audience.

I agree with the spirit of these theological moves but would amend the older approaches to accommodation with three modern observations; I would also advise an adjustment to the traditional nomenclature.

First, as understood by these earlier Christians, the human authors of Scripture were colluding partners in the act of accommodation. In Calvin's account, for instance, we find that not only God, but also Moses, knew but kept secret the proper scientific cosmology.[7] So God *and* Moses accommodated their discourse to the confused Israelites. In contrast to this view, I would argue that accommodation did not occur between Scripture's human author and audience but rather between God and the human author himself. God *adopted* the author of Genesis as *his* author and, in doing so, adopted that human author's ancient view of the cosmos; God knew the right cosmology, but neither "Moses" nor the Israelites did.

My second amendment regarding accommodation would be its extent. Earlier Christians appealed to accommodation only at certain points, where Scripture seemed mistaken or when, logically speaking, it addressed theological concerns that were simply beyond the limits of human comprehension.[8] I would argue instead that *all* Scripture is accom-

---

6. For a good introduction to the concept of accommodation in the church fathers and Judaism, see Stephen D. Benin, *The Footprints of God: Divine Accommodation in Jewish and Christian Thought* (Albany: State University of New York Press, 1993).

7. John Calvin, *Commentaries on the First Book of Moses, called Genesis,* tr. John King (2 vols.; Edinburgh: Calvin Translation Society, 1847-50), 1.79-80.

8. This view also shows up in some modern theology, which tries to distinguish between

modated discourse for the very reason that, on every page of Scripture, God has *adopted* the words and viewpoints of finite, fallen human authors as the words and viewpoints of his holy book: the entire Bible is accommodated discourse.[9] And this is why God's book includes all things native to human discourse — truth and error, good and bad, righteousness and things unrighteous: one finds all this in the Bible.

Third, I would suggest that we avoid a possible implication of the word "accommodation" by substituting the concept of "providential adoption." Although accommodation language has a long-standing pedigree in the Christian theological tradition, the notion has at least one serious disadvantage.[10] "Accommodation" tends to anthropomorphically connote God's *active* role in communicating errant human viewpoints for the purposes of revelation, but I suspect that a more nuanced account should honor the human will by making this more passive. That is, in inscripturation God allowed his human authors the freedom to be precisely who they were when they wrote Scripture. If this is right, then we err if we characterize every "biblical problem" as God's wise rhetorical strategy to reach some greater spiritual end. It is better to say that, in the process of reaching a greater end, the humans involved in writing Scripture inevitably showed their true colors, including their errors and sins. Such a "passive" account of the matter is particularly important in the case of biblical genocide (and similar textual terrors), else we are compelled to say that God participated in human evils to achieve a grander spiritual purpose. A better description in these cases would be that God has canonically *adopted* human authors as his speakers and that, in doing so, he has permitted these authors — fallen as they were — to write the sorts of things that ancient, fallen people would write about their enemies. It is one of the great myster-

---

what is "accommodated" and what is altogether true. See Peter van Inwagen, "Genesis and Evolution," in *Reasoned Faith*, ed. E. Stump (Ithaca, NY: Cornell University Press, 1993), 93-127.

9. Here following the insightful thesis of Nicholas Wolterstorff, *Divine Discourse: Philosophical Reflections on the Claim That God Speaks* (Cambridge: Cambridge University Press, 1995). See also Karl Barth, *Church Dogmatics* (Edinburgh: T. & T. Clark, 1936-77), 1/2.509.

10. These are pointed out in Eric Seibert's theological critique of the approach to accommodation in my *God's Word in Human Words: An Evangelical Appropriation of Critical Biblical Scholarship* (Grand Rapids: Baker, 2008). See Eric A. Seibert, *Disturbing Divine Behavior: Troubling Old Testament Images of God* (Minneapolis: Fortress, 2009), 270-72.

ies of faith that God's redemptive activity is carried out successfully and beautifully through the agency of fallen men and women.

Lest we create the impression that God is merely passive in the writing of Scripture, I would add that a good theology of adoption depends to some extent on the venerable doctrine of *providence,* a belief that God is active in ordering creaturely realities to their proper ends.[11] Numerous biblical texts advance this doctrine. One naturally thinks of Paul's claim that "God works all things together for good" (Rom 8:28), but the strongest witnesses are biblical narratives, like the stories of Joseph, Ruth, and Esther, whose authors artfully taught that God is at work in mundane human circumstances. As this applies to our theology of Scripture, we will say that God, in adopting human texts as his own, was involved both in the production of the texts and in their canonical adoption as sacred Scripture. Precisely how God did this while allowing room for everything human — including choice, success, error, goodness, and sin — is not something that we can explicate. But this is indeed how it seems to have worked.

My preference for "providential adoption" over "accommodation" aside, the general contours of my approach to the problem of Scripture stand fairly close to what we sometimes find in the writings of the church fathers and Calvin. My point is not that Calvin, Gregory, and Justin were necessarily correct in everything they said, nor that they would agree with all of my proposals. Rather, my main point is that faithful Christians of the past have suggested already some of the things that I am suggesting here. That Scripture itself is in need of redemption — that it contains "laws not good" which God will in time redeem — is not wholly foreign to the Christian (or Jewish) tradition. The thesis is worthy of a serious consideration. In my opinion, it is a better explication of the "dark side" of Scripture than an approach that seeks to harmonize Gospel love and genocide as theologically compatible ideas. There is no such thing as Martin Luther's "severe mercy," which combined the violence of Deuteronomy and love of Jesus to justify the persecution of Jews "for their own good."[12]

---

11. John Webster, *Holy Scripture: A Dogmatic Sketch* (Cambridge: University Press, 2003), 10.

12. Martin Luther, "On the Jews and Their Lies," in *Luther's Works* 47, ed. F. Sherman (55 vols.; Philadelphia: Fortress, 1971), 268-74, 285-92 (137-306). For his uses of the concept of "severe mercy" *(scharfe Barmherzigkeit),* see pp. 268, 272, 292.

A second question that might be raised about my proposal regards the nature of Scripture's "inspiration." In what sense is Scripture "from God"? In responses to an earlier and longer book that I have written on the subject of Scripture, some reviewers expressed surprise that the book did not offer a more explicit account and description of inspiration. Here I will try to do modestly better, though it will become clear that I simply do not believe that there is much that we *can* say about it if the goal is to actually describe the process and its nature.

Discussions of inspiration often begin with Scripture's explicit comments about itself, especially with texts like 2 Tim 3:16 and 2 Pet 1:20-21. Though I will do this as well, this important exegetical procedure is not a foolproof guide to good bibliology. The biblical authors did not necessarily have anything like a comprehensive doctrine of Scripture, and they lived long before the advent of, and insights derived from, biblical criticism and the so-called "linguistic turn" in postmodern philosophy. Even if the New Testament authors were to have said something like "God dictated the law to Moses word-for-word" or "the human authors of Scripture never erred," these things could not be right if we take them at face value because there is so much other evidence that must be considered. So, while we should read and take seriously the biblical testimony about Scripture, the actual phenomena of Scripture and our modern philosophical insights about hermeneutics and epistemology must also figure in our theological deliberations about inspiration.

Scripture is commonly described as "inspired," an English translation of *theopneustos*, the Greek word in 2 Tim 3:16 often characterized as meaning "God-breathed." Surely this was one way of saying that the Old Testament came from God and hence that it is God's authoritative word, but the Greek word itself does not really imply anything in particular about *how* the transaction between God and the human authors took place. It is possible that the author's understanding of inspiration (whether Paul or someone else) went no deeper than this, but even if he knew more, he has left it unsaid. The author goes on to describe the benefits of Scripture for Christian teaching and spiritual formation, but this does not bear directly on the question of inspiration.

Theologians generally turn next to the short text in 2 Pet 1:20-21, which tells us that "no prophecy [of Scripture] ever came by the will of man, but men borne by the Holy Spirit spoke from God." Here the focus is not on the inspired *text* (as in 2 Timothy) but rather on the inspired *authors,* who were "borne" or "carried along" by the Holy Spirit.[13] Again, the passage offers minimal detail, but we can infer at least one point with some confidence. When the author emphasizes the Spirit's role in "carrying along" the biblical writers and denies that their "wills" were involved, this seems to reflect a *dictation theory* of inscripturation, according to which God's human authors were essentially his stenographers.[14] This theory of inspiration was very common (in fact, the rule) in early paganism, Judaism, and Christianity,[15] but modern Christians, including even some very conservative Christians, would no longer accept this description of inspiration. The human authors were more "involved" in writing Scripture than dictation will allow. So whatever the author of 2 Peter had in mind with his idea that the biblical writers were "carried along" by the Spirit, we cannot take it as conclusive evidence for a theologically detailed description of inspiration. It will bear only the more general point that the Holy Spirit was somehow at work in the biblical authors. I would certainly not try to build a doctrine of inspiration on this text, as is commonly done in some conservative theological circles.[16] The insight that can be gleaned from this text is fairly modest.[17]

Now it is quite possible that the author of 2 Peter was referring only to the Old Testament prophets in his comments on inspiration. The prophetic books make the strongest case for a kind of dictation in the process of inscripturation. Their ubiquitous mantra, "Thus says the LORD," reflex-

13. Cf. Heb 3:7 and 10:15, which refer either to the Holy Spirit as the author of the Old Testament or, more likely, to the Spirit using the Old Testament to speak to the author's audience.

14. Charles Bigg, *A Critical and Exegetical Commentary on the Epistles of St. Peter and St. Jude* (ICC; Edinburgh: T. & T. Clark, 1969), 269-70.

15. Implied already in Clement of Alexandria's *Protrepticus* 9, in Gregory of Nazianzus's *Oration* 2.105, and in Philo's *Moses* 1.283. Clearer still are Augustine, in *De Consensu evangelistarum* 1.54, and Gregory the Great in *Moralia* 1.2. For discussion, see Barth, *Church Dogmatics,* 1/2.517-26.

16. Carl F. H. Henry, *God, Revelation, and Authority* (6 vols.; Waco, TX: Word, 1976-83), 4.132-61.

17. For a more realistic approach, see the short treatment of this text in Webster's *Holy Scripture: A Dogmatic Sketch,* 36-39.

ively identifies the prophetic words as the very words of Yahweh. But again, there are difficulties. In the case of Ezekiel, for instance, the prophet announced that Tyre would fall to Nebuchadnezzar of Babylon (ch. 26), but three chapters later he admitted that those words, though introduced with the customary "Thus says the LORD" formula, did not and apparently would not come to pass (29:17-20). If one knows something about ancient Israelite history, many similar but more subtle problems of "failed prophecy" appear elsewhere in the prophetic corpus. The problem became so acute in later Judaism that (according to most scholars) the little book of Jonah was written to explain why some prophetic announcements of judgment did not come to pass.[18] In saying this, I do not intend to cast doubt on the callings and ministries of the biblical prophets. I only mean to point out that human judgment was sufficiently involved in their oracles to preclude any simple, straightforward notion of dictation.

To these observations about inspiration we can add that, when we consider the Bible as a whole, the processes that produced Scripture were surprisingly diverse. Some biblical authors wrote history through research and the consultation of sources (e.g., 1-2 Kings and Luke-Acts), another philosophized about the vanity of life (Ecclesiastes), some were given visions (Revelation) or prophetic words (Isaiah), and others wrote personal letters (Paul) or spoke very candidly of personal feelings and frustrations (Psalms and Job). The whole matter becomes quite fascinating and puzzling if one thinks much about it. I believe that Stephen Chapman is right when he describes *inspiration* as "a cipher for a mysterious process of divine-human co-writing."[19] In the end, we simply do not understand how it worked. Inspiration affirms that the Bible is God's authoritative word and that we should read it with seriousness, but conceptually speaking this does not tell us with precision either *what* we should expect from the Bible or *how* we should read it.

Moreover, if we wish to discuss inspiration more comprehensively, I

18. Brevard S. Childs, *Introduction to the Old Testament as Scripture* (Philadelphia: Fortress, 1979), 417-27; J. Alberto Soggin, *Introduction to the Old Testament* (Louisville: Westminster/John Knox, 1989), 414-19.

19. Stephen B. Chapman, "Reclaiming Inspiration for the Bible," in *Canon and Biblical Interpretation*, ed. C. G. Bartholomew, et al. (Scripture and Hermeneutics Series 7; Grand Rapids: Zondervan, 2006), 167 (167-206).

think that we will soon find ourselves dealing with the more arcane and complex subject of "revelation."[20] Does "revelation" describe only those instances in which God freely discloses *himself* to human beings, as some (especially Barthian) theologians argue, or can we speak as well of "words," "ideas," or "concepts" that are revealed to human beings in Scripture? Is revelation irresistibly effective, so that everyone who receives it responds truly and appropriately, or is it possible that human beings can perceive, modestly understand, and then finally reject revelation from God? Does revelation always break into the created order from the outside, or might it originate on the inside and point outward? These are heady questions that I cannot tackle in this limited space, though I think that one can deduce something of what I think about revelation, natural theology, and irresistible grace from what I have written here. But these important questions aside, I believe that what I have said already entails something important about revelation and inspiration.

In Scripture, God speaks to us through the finite and fallen perspectives of human authors and, thereby, through the limited and fallen horizons of human cultures and audiences. And the process whereby he accomplished this was and is very human, both in the production of the individual biblical books themselves and in the lengthy historical process — both Jewish and Christian — that finally produced our respective canons of Scripture (Jewish, Catholic, Orthodox, and Protestant).[21] Just as God's providential and creative hand was in the long and convoluted evolutionary processes that produced human lives and souls, so his hand was in the complex historical process that produced Holy Scripture. It is difficult to go much beyond this in explicating the theological details of inspiration and inscripturation. We see the matter "through a mirror dimly" (1 Cor 13:12). And in the end, I think that our grasping after a metaphor for inspiration turns out to be mainly academic. For regardless of the manner

20. For several different but valuable discussions, see William J. Abraham, *Crossing the Threshold of Divine Revelation* (Grand Rapids: Eerdmans, 2006); Avery Robert Dulles, *Models of Revelation* (Maryknoll, NY: Orbis, 1992); Colin E. Gunton, *A Brief Theology of Revelation* (Edinburgh: T & T Clark, 1995); and Richard Swinburne, *From Metaphor to Analogy* (Oxford: Clarendon, 1992).

21. For a recent discussion, see Craig Allert, *A High View of Scripture? The Authority of the Bible and the Formation of the New Testament Canon* (Grand Rapids: Baker, 2007).

in which God gave us Scripture, the end result is the text that we have before us. And our interpretation of that text and its message is not deeply affected by the divine activity that created Scripture, whatever this may have been.

Third, another pressing question, especially for my own evangelical community: If we admit that Scripture, as the word of God, includes error and has been influenced by human sin, how can it possibly serve an authoritative role in the church? How can we know where God speaks and where humans have spoken? And how can we distinguish biblical truth from error? I will answer this question in more detail in chapter 8, but to this line of questioning I would offer several preliminary remarks.

Let us first take note of the fact that the Bible is *not* a human necessity. As Paul pointed out in Romans, those without a written Bible are responsible to the moral law written on the heart. Human beings who lived before the Bible was written or who now live without one must "make the best of it" in the effort to render and live out their ethical judgments. God will judge them equitably on that basis. So neither they nor anyone else *needs* a Bible, much less an inerrant Bible, to be accountable before God's authority and to be treated fairly and justly by God. To be sure, those with Scripture at hand are in a *potentially* better situation for making theological and ethical judgments, but the interpretive context of human ethics and morality does not change dramatically simply because we bring Scripture into it. This is in part because biblical interpreters are finite and fallen people, and in part because Scripture itself was written by finite, fallen authors. Given that this is the case, it is apparently very easy (as *all* of us well know) for fallen people to legitimize sin and vice through appeals to Scripture.

Another point that I would make along these lines is that biblical authority does not seem to require biblical perfection. Scripture itself recognizes or establishes numerous "authorities" (governments, church leaders, parents, etc.) who are imperfect but legitimate in God's eyes. Perfection is not a necessary or even possible quality in good parents, presidents or pastors. At best these authorities are fallible people who, on the whole, foster and promote what is good and healthy for those under their care and direction. This was aptly expressed by Bishop Ignatius (c. 115), who counseled Christians to accept the bishop "as the Lord himself" but admitted that "I am not giving you orders as if I were someone. . . . For now I have merely begun to be a disciple and am speaking to you as my fellow learners."[22] The Apostle Paul seems to have had similar ideas. He confessed his human limitations but did not believe that these compromised his authority over his churches.[23]

In his wisdom, God has ordained that fallible human beings will serve as authorities for the thriving of human life. The same can be said of Scripture's authority. It need not be a perfect book to serve as God's useful, healthy, and authoritative guide to truth and spiritual insight. Scripture fills its role by saying *clearly enough* that our human condition is in need of redemption and that God has moved in Christ to redeem us. By virtue of its human form and character, Scripture is an *adequate human voice* that does not fare so well when judged by the yardstick of divine perfection. Rightly understood, the Bible advances our understanding of the human situation beyond what we gain from life experience alone. It is "special revelation," but it does not take us to the epistemic end or to anything like a full or complete understanding of God and the human situation. A complete and comprehensive book about God, humanity, and the cosmos would undoubtedly be much larger than the Bible and, even if it existed, no human being could really understand it. God is our ultimate authority, and he mediates this authority to us through creaturely means, including through a book written and assembled by human beings.

A fourth question might be this: If Scripture is such as I have described, if it is indeed a casualty of our fallen situation, then why, in the end, should we believe that it is God's word at all? How is it "God's word" any more than the Islamic Qur'an or the Hindu Bhagavad-Gita? Though this is not an apologetic book that "defends" our belief in Scripture, I admit that the question deserves to be addressed, if briefly. I would approach the matter from two different directions.

On the one hand, I would say that God's word has never been limited to Scripture alone. Scripture itself tells us that creation speaks a word from God to all men (Psalm 19; cf. Rom 10:18) and depicts God speaking to

---

22. Ignatius, *Ephesians* 3, 6 (Bart D. Ehrman, *The Apostolic Fathers*, vol. 1 [LCL 24; Cambridge: Harvard University Press, 2003], 223, 225).

23. Cf. Rom 11:33-36; 1 Cor 4:4; 2 Cor 10:8; 13:10; 1 Thess 2:13.

numerous people without Scripture, on one occasion to Gentile magicians through superstitious astrology (Matthew 2).[24] If Karl Barth was right to aver that God can speak to us "through a dead dog or a communist" — and I think that he certainly was right about this — then there is no good reason to deny that God has spoken to people through books besides the Bible — not only through "spiritual classics" of the Christian faith but also through the Hindu Gitas and Islamic Qur'an.[25] When a Muslim refrains from murder on account of the Qur'an's command, "Do not kill" (Sura 6.151), who is it that speaks rightly to the Muslim conscience except God himself? So I freely admit that my description of Scripture makes it one of many instances in which God speaks to a fallen world through fallen human discourse.

But let us approach the question from the other direction. It is a matter of Christian dogma that the Bible is especially God's written word. What makes Scripture unique among religious books? How is it the "word of God" in a way that the Qur'an never is or will be? This question is often answered by appeal to the doctrine of inspiration, so that Scripture is ontologically unique because it is "God-breathed," but I have already pointed out that this approach is not uncomplicated. Luke (for instance) seems oblivious to the fact that he was writing Scripture, and in Paul's case he explicitly contrasted a brief "word from the Lord" with *his* words to Corinth in the rest of the letter (1 Cor 7:10-12).[26] So in giving an account of Scripture's uniqueness, I would say that the Bible's special status as God's inspired word stems, not so much from the unusual spiritual experiences of its authors (whatever those were), but rather from

---

24. Cardinal Joseph Ratzinger, *Truth and Tolerance: Christian Belief and World Religions*, tr. H. Taylor (San Francisco: Ignatius, 2003), 20.

25. Here I paraphrase from Barth's *Church Dogmatics*, 1/1.60.

26. Paul's comments are sometimes construed to say that his entire book was "the Lord's word," excepting his own parenthetical comment in 7:12ff. But a careful examination of his rhetoric shows that this is not at all the point. Paul writes seven chapters before he introduces a comment as from "the Lord," after which he immediately returns to his own discourse ("I, not the Lord"; see Gordon D. Fee, *The First Epistle to the Corinthians* [Grand Rapids: Eerdmans, 1987], 290-96). Paul certainly viewed himself as a speaker and writer of God's word (see 1 Cor 14:37; 1 Thess 2:13), but this does not mean that he viewed himself as an inspired author of Scripture akin to Moses or Isaiah. Only later, but not very much later, did Christians begin to accept his letters as Scripture (2 Pet 3:15).

its divinely-ordained relationship to the incarnate word. By God's design, Jewish Scripture pointed forward to the appearance of Jesus the Messiah, while Christian Scripture reflects back on his appearance by testifying to it, drawing out its implications, and preparing the way for the parousia, for that final moment when, according to Scripture, Christ will return and put all things right. Nowhere is this point about Christ's relationship to Scripture more vividly pressed home than in John's Gospel: "You search the Scriptures because you think that in them you have eternal life, but it is they that bear witness to me, yet you refuse to come to me that you may have life" (John 5:39-40). Scripture is not an end in itself. It points to God's work in Christ, "testifying" or "bearing witness" to the good news of the Messiah. For this reason, Scripture may properly be called "Holy Scripture" (Rom 1:2; 2 Tim 3:15), insofar as it is a book that has been "sanctified" and "set apart" by God for its unique role in the economy of salvation.[27] Inspiration is mysterious. But the book created by it reveals "the mystery of godliness," namely that Jesus Christ "was manifested in the flesh, vindicated in the Spirit, seen by angels, preached among the nations, believed on in the world, taken up in glory" (1 Tim 3:16).

Another (fifth) question about my thesis will be this one: If we admit that Scripture is a casualty of the Fall and that its pages sometimes include astonishingly troubling thoughts and ideas, will this not cause some believers to doubt the Bible's status as God's word and some non-believers to flatly reject it?

Yes, that will sometimes be the effect. Just as some people doubt God's existence and goodness because of the trouble in our broken world, so there will always be those who construe the "problems" in Scripture as evidence that the Bible simply cannot be God's written word. But of course, Christians should disagree with this logic. Just as we embrace our broken world as the good creation of a good God, so we embrace the broken text of Scripture as God's good word. We are not unduly distracted by Scripture's brokenness because its truth and beauty, like a sunset and a child's smile, remind us that it comes from the good hand of a good God. The Bible is a sacred word that testifies to the truly wonderful things that

---

27. See Webster, *Holy Scripture: A Dogmatic Sketch*, 17-41.

God has done and is doing to mend our broken world. Foremost, it testifies to what God has done for us in Christ. If Christ has been raised, then the broken Bible that points to him is uniquely God's word; if he has not been raised, then the Bible turns out to be just another broken, religious book.[28]

I would argue, too, that facing up to the problems in Scripture is more likely to help than hurt the gospel at this point. We live in a post-Christian and pluralistic world that is increasingly sensitive to the ethics of human equality (largely because of Christian influence!). Christians themselves, not to mention skeptics, are increasingly troubled by the dark side of Scripture. Preaching the "good news" will become progressively more difficult if we continue to argue that the slavery, ethnic profiling, genocide, and religious persecutions advocated or permitted in Scripture are actually "good laws" from God. These things are not good; they are "laws not good" as Ezekiel put it, laws that reflect our "hardness of heart" as Christ expressed it (Ezek 20:25; Matt 19:8). Christ's message and work and the ministry of his Spirit are redemptively putting this brokenness behind us.

Finally, one more question. If we admit that Scripture is as I have described, does this not open up the door to an "anything goes" theology that interprets Scripture so that it says nice things that we like? Will we simply pick and choose as "final" those texts that suit our fancies? Indeed, there is a tendency in all of us to twist and contort Scripture so that it condones and reinforces our pet views and vices. A worst-case scenario comes from Nazi Germany, where Christian sympathizers interpreted the biblical Jesus as an anti-Semitic Nazi,[29] but all Christians succumb in some way or other to this threat. To see how true this is, one only needs to notice that, even among Fundamentalists who deny the human error in Scripture, one finds a wide variety of conflicting "inerrantist" readings. Some inerrantists claim that the Bible clearly teaches "predestination," others that it clearly teaches "free will." Some inerrantists argue that Scripture strongly supports "infant baptism," while others believe that it obviously teaches "believer's baptism." Some inerrantists are "pacifists," while

28. Cf. 1 Cor 15:12-19.

29. See Richard Steigmann-Gall, *The Holy Reich: Nazi Conceptions of Christianity, 1919-1945* (Cambridge: University Press, 2003).

others advocate "just war" theory. No approach to Scripture, whether hermeneutical or theological, will prevent us from badly misreading it at points. But this much is certain: in the end, the success of biblical interpretation depends a great deal on whether we want to listen to God or merely tell him what he ought to say. For it is only by listening to God — to what he says in *all* of Scripture, and through all avenues by which he might speak, such as the voices of the Spirit and of creation — that we can finally arrive at the best understanding of how the Spirit is directing us to love God and our neighbor.

CHAPTER 7

The Redemption of Scripture:
Biblical Examples

S cripture is a casualty of the fallen cosmos. I have adduced evidence
for this assertion by highlighting numerous tensions and contradictions in the Bible, including ethical tensions, and by demonstrating that
some of the best-known church leaders in history have admitted that
Scripture indeed reflects divine accommodations to humanity's fallen
condition. But if these assertions are theologically valid, then we should
be able to adduce direct and explicit biblical evidence that Scripture is in
need of redemption and that God is working to redeem it. I believe that
this evidence is readily available in Scripture. Numerous examples could
be cited, but here I will refer mainly to examples from the Gospel of Matthew. I will then supplement these observations with an example from
the Old Testament.

To my mind, the best example of "redeemed Scripture" is the way Jesus casts his teachings in contrast to the Old Testament law in his Sermon
on the Mount (Matthew 5–7). Here are some examples:

> It was also said [by Moses], "Whoever divorces his wife, let him give her
> a certificate of divorce." But I say to you that anyone who divorces his
> wife, except on the ground of unchastity, causes her to commit adul-
> tery; and whoever marries a divorced woman commits adultery. (Matt
> 5:31-32)

You have heard that it was said [by Moses], "An eye for an eye and a
tooth for a tooth." But I say to you, Do not resist an evildoer. But if anyone strikes you on the right cheek, turn the other also. (vv. 38-39)

You have heard that it was said [by Moses], "You shall love your neighbor and hate your enemy." But I say to you, Love your enemies and pray
for those who persecute you. (vv. 43-44)[1]

In all three instances Jesus quotes or alludes to the law of Moses and then
offers, as his own teaching, something that negates or reverses the law.
He takes a particularly strong stand against the law's violent streak, such
as its demand that Israel return evil for evil in legal cases or kill its
Canaanite enemies. The sermon appeared so contrary to the law that Jesus had to add a word of clarification: "Do not think that I have come to
abolish the law or the prophets; I have come not to abolish but to fulfill"
(Matt 5:17). Though we are Christians and of course believe him on this
point, we cannot help but ask: How can it be that Jesus fulfills the law by
reversing its teachings?

We can answer this question by attending closely to another text in
Matthew's Gospel. In one of his confrontations with Jewish leaders, Jesus
repeated and expanded on his teaching that divorce was unacceptable,
even if the law of Moses permitted it. We have at our disposal both the
challenge of Jewish leaders and Jesus' thoughtful response to them:

They said to him, "Why then did Moses command us to give a certifi-
cate of dismissal and to divorce her?" He said to them, "It was because
you were so hard-hearted that Moses allowed you to divorce your
wives, but from the beginning it was not so." (19:7-8)

According to Jesus, in this case at least, the law of Moses did not offer the
Jews a path for healthy living. It offered instead a civil regulation designed

1. Conservative theologians uncomfortable with the Bible's theological diversity often
argue that the Old Testament law does not actually say "hate your enemy," which is techni-
cally true but essentially wrong. It does command Israel to have "no compassion" on its enemies and to annihilate them, including innocent children and animals. That is hatred, and
obviously so.

for hardhearted, unspiritual persons.[2] Paradoxically, in this case fulfillment of the law amounted to what Keith Ward has called sublation, that is, reversal or negation of the law.[3] Hence, while it is true that Jesus did not come to abolish the law, the actual result in some cases was the law's abolishment. As the author of Ephesians put it, Christ made peace "by abolishing in his flesh the law of commandments and ordinances" (Eph 2:15). Paul Ricoeur combines the testimony of Christ and Ephesians when he points out that in Christ "the novelty abolishes the Scripture *and* fulfills it."[4]

A more striking example of the redemption of Scripture is provided by the Gospel of Matthew as a whole. Like other early Christians, Matthew viewed Jesus as the "new Moses" prophesied in Deut 18:15: "Yahweh your God will raise up for you a prophet like me from among your own brothers. You must listen to him."[5] This is why the life of Matthew's Jesus closely parallels the life of Israel's ancient lawgiver.[6] Like Moses, Jesus was born as a savior. Like Moses, a foreign king tried to kill him. Like Moses, Jesus was hidden from the threatening king in Egypt. Like Moses, Jesus fasted in the desert wilderness for forty days and nights. Like Moses, Jesus returned from that desert experience and taught God's people on the mountain. And in that Sermon on the Mount he presented his teaching as a new law that reversed and fulfilled the law of Moses. Also, in Matthew as

2. To be clear, I do not believe that the human author of Deuteronomy viewed his divorce law as an accommodation to human depravity. If the law was so intended, it was by God and not by the ancient legist he adopted to write Scripture. Whether Jesus himself recognized this subtle distinction between human and divine agency I cannot say.

3. Keith Ward, *What the Bible Really Teaches: A Challenge for Fundamentalists* (London: SPCK, 2004), 23.

4. Italics added. See Paul Ricoeur, *Essays on Biblical Interpretation* (Philadelphia: Fortress, 1980), 50.

5. For an early Christian text, see Acts 3:21-26; 7:20-39. Origen and Augustine also saw Jesus as the fulfillment of this prophecy (see in Joseph T. Lienhard, *Exodus, Leviticus, Numbers, Deuteronomy* [ACCS; Downers Grove, IL: InterVarsity, 2001], 304). For similar messianic readings of Deut 18:15 among Samaritans and Jews, see John Lierman, *The New Testament Moses: Christian perceptions of Moses and Israel in the Setting of Jewish Religion* (WUNT2 173; Tübingen: Mohr Siebeck, 2004), 86-89, 279-82.

6. The standard discussion is Dale C. Allison, Jr., *The New Moses: A Matthean Typology* (Minneapolis: Fortress, 1993). See also Pope Benedict XVI, *Jesus of Nazareth: From the Baptism in the Jordan to the Transfiguration*, tr. A. J. Walker (New York: Doubleday, 2007), 66.

a whole, the teaching of Jesus is presented in five sections, each ending with the words "When Jesus had finished saying these things."[7] This structure parallels the five books of Moses that stand at the beginning of the Old Testament. Once we realize that this was Matthew's intention — to present Jesus as the new Moses of prophecy — then we are in a better position to appreciate the conclusion of his Gospel in Matt 28:16-20, commonly known as the "Great Commission."

Readers will probably recall that, because of his sin, Moses was not able to lead the Israelites into the Promised Land.[8] At the end of his life, he stood on a mountain overlooking the land and said to the Israelites, "I cannot go with you, but God will be with you. . . . *Go, and kill all the nations.*"[9] This parallels very closely what we find at the end of Matthew's Gospel. Jesus takes his disciples "to the mountain" and there speaks his own final words: "*Go, make disciples of all the nations . . . and I will be with you.*" It is quite clear that Matthew wished to portray Jesus as a better Moses, who, because he was sinless, could address his followers *from within the land* and could extend the promise to be with them in their mission. Particularly striking, of course, is the profound contrast between the two missions: "kill all the nations" (Greek *panta ta ethnē*); "make disciples of all the nations" (again *panta ta ethnē*). Matthew apparently means to teach us that the true fulfillment of the command to kill the Canaanites is actually found in our efforts to convert the lost to faith in Christ. The Gospel is thus understood as a spiritual conquest in the name of Christ and for the good of the nations. So the Gospel of Matthew is a deliberate and sustained attempt to redeem the Old Testament law and make it serve the purposes of the Gospel of Jesus Christ.

Modern Christians are not the only ones who have been troubled by the Old Testament's command to exterminate the Canaanites. Jesus himself and/or his biographer Matthew were also concerned about this problem and worked in their redemptive missions to reverse the dangerous, genocidal message found in Deuteronomy. According to these New Testa-

---

7. See Matt 7:28-29; 11:1; 13:53; 19:1-2; 26:1-2.

8. This discussion is drawn from my well-received article, "Gospel as Conquest: Mosaic Typology in Matthew 28:16-20," CBQ 68 (2006): 651-63.

9. See LXX Deut 11:23; Josh 23:4; 24:18.

SACRED WORD, BROKEN WORD

ment sources, the Old Testament law participates in the broken state of human affairs and is thereby a vivid portrait of our need of redemption; it follows that *fulfillment* of the law will entail not only predicted blessings but also a complete reversal of the law's broken, violent, and dangerous elements.

These observations seem to cast negative light on the Old Testament and to reinforce a perception in popular thought, and even in some scholarly circles, that the New Testament redeems the Old, that "the letter kills, but the spirit gives life," so to speak (see 2 Cor 3:6). While there is obviously *some* truth in this perception, as a simple statement of fact it is wrong and must be qualified in various ways.

First, such a view runs counter to biblical practice. When Paul referred to the "letter that kills," he had in mind only those parts of the Old Testament that presented special problems. This is why he and other early Christians could comfortably appeal to the Old Testament as support for their views of theology and ethics. In fact, the Old Testament provided the basis for Christianity's most profound redemptive messages. The Gospel command to love God, neighbor, and enemy was not invented by Jesus but was drawn directly from the Hebrew Bible (see Deut 6:5; Lev 19:18; Prov 25:21-22). In fact, the whole idea of a Messianic "New Covenant" was proffered in the Old Testament long before the New Testament authors took up their pens. So the highest and best of biblical theology and ethics is expressed in both testaments.

Second, there are numerous instances in which the Old Testament authors themselves worked to redeem the broken portraits in Scripture. Consider, for example, these parallel Old Testament texts:

Again the anger of *Yahweh* was kindled against Israel, and he incited David against them, saying, "Go, number Israel and Judah." (2 Sam 24:1)

Satan stood up against Israel, and incited David to number Israel. (1 Chron 21:1)

While these texts undoubtedly refer to the same census taken by King David, the respective authors oppose each other when it comes to the spiritual agent behind the census. The earlier author believed that *God* moved the king to count his fighting men, whereas the later author of Chronicles worked to allay this misconception by attributing the motivation to Satan. In making this move, the Chronicler sought to redeem an earlier theological portrait of God that he found objectionable. A similar move was made by the author of Job, who wrote to allay the impression, fostered in many of the Proverbs, that human suffering is always caused by sin. This, he tells us, is simply not the case. So the Old Testament, no less than the New, includes redemptive theological insight.

Third, we should note that even the New Testament, in spite of its special position and redemptive role in the canon, is by no means fully redeemed. It still envisions slavery as an acceptable social practice, maintains a very low view of women at points, and throws ethnic slurs at Cretans. So the authors of both testaments were human beings who lived and wrote "within certain limits and therefore relatively they are all vulnerable and therefore capable of error even in respect of religion and theology."[10] We cannot carelessly pit one biblical author against another, as if one had it all right and another was all wrong. Each author spoke for God in a particular way.

The Bible, with its two testaments, plays a vital role in God's redemptive work. Taken as a whole it is a steady and valuable guide for God's people as they seek to know him and to love their neighbors. But ultimately, the redemption of both testaments, and of the cosmos and humanity, is accomplished by the death, burial, resurrection, ascension, and return of Jesus Christ. Until that final day arrives, we will continue to struggle with the problems of pain and suffering, and with the problems in Scripture. These are *our* problems that God has graciously taken upon himself in Jesus Christ.

---

10. Karl Barth, *Church Dogmatics* (Edinburgh: T. & T. Clark, 1936-77), 1/2.510.

CHAPTER 8

Christian Epistemology:
Broken Readers of Sacred Scripture

If this is the nature of Scripture — that it is an *adequate and useful* book written from fallible human perspectives and includes diverse and sometimes conflicting viewpoints on the same subjects — and if we ourselves, as readers of Scripture, are in turn fallible readers, how can we know when our interpretations of Scripture are correct? And how can we be certain that we have arrived at the proper theological conclusions? The simple answer is "We cannot." As is the case when we read any text, when we read the Bible there is the *possibility* of understanding and, in most cases, the likelihood of *some* understanding. But we do not achieve anything like a perfect "God's eye" perspective on the world, on ourselves, on others, or on God. In fact, success is never assured when we read Scripture. Many are the Christians who have read the Bible and, on that very basis, confidently decided to kill anyone of a different ethnicity, nationality, or religious persuasion. As one American colonist put it after annihilating a group of Native Americans: "Sometimes Scripture declareth women and children must perish with their parents. . . . We had sufficient light from the Word of God for our proceedings. . . . It was a fearful sight to see them frying in the fire, with streams of blood quenching it; the smell was horrible, but the victory seemed a sweet sacrifice."[1]

---

1. Cited from Ben Kiernan, *Blood and Soil: A World History of Genocide and Extermination from Sparta to Darfur* (New Haven: Yale University Press, 2007), 231.

Obviously we hope to do much better, but we know only too well that all of us, you and I, err in some respects when we try to read and live out Scripture. Given this reality — that Scripture is broken and that we are broken — it is fairly easy to see that there is no such thing as foolproof human knowledge, even if that knowledge supposedly comes from thoughtful prayer and from a close and careful reading of God's written word. If this seems to present an intractable problem for biblical authority, if we are tempted to say in response, "Why read the Bible or take it seriously?" then I would suggest that we have poorly understood what human knowledge is and, on that improper basis, have construed wrongly how Scripture ought to serve its authoritative role.

This line of questioning brings us into that wing of philosophy called epistemology, which studies the nature of human knowledge. What is knowledge? How do we get it? What conditions make it possible? When does belief become knowledge? These are the kinds of questions that epistemology explores.

As we begin a discussion of epistemology and interpretation, I should make clear where my interest lies. Human beings lay claim to different kinds of knowledge. For example, "1 + 1 = 2," "the fire truck is red," and "Paul believed in salvation by faith" constitute very different kinds of propositions. Here I am not interested in anything as simple as "1 + 1 = 2" or "the fire truck is red." These are matters of logic and simple perception. My main interest is whether and how human interpretations of things like history, literature, philosophy, psychology, culture, religion, and theology (as examples) can be true. In what ways did Ezekiel and Paul actually understand things divine and human, and to what extent can we, as later readers of their books, grasp what these biblical authors said?

It is probably obvious by now that I am espousing a particular understanding of epistemology, which believes the human capacity for knowledge is *potentially adequate*. Both words — *potentially* and *adequate* — are important, inasmuch as I intend to say that human interpretations yield knowledge that is at best adequate and never perfect, and that in some cases our interpretations are not even adequate for the task. But in the best cases, human knowledge is sufficient to allow for the spiritual, psychological, and social thriving of human beings. At this point I would like to explain why this sort of epistemology — let us call it *Practical Realism* — is the preferable Christian view of human knowledge. And I would like to do so by casting the discussion in terms of various types of epistemology and their respective places in history. These (5) types include: *Tacit Realism, Reflective Realism, Modern Realism, Postmodern Antirealism,* and *Postmodern Practical Realism.* Let us consider each in turn.

Tacit and Reflective Realism

Tacit Realism could also be called Simple Realism, in that it is the unstated, unexamined epistemology of every person in every age of history — of old and young, of educated and uneducated, of Jew and Greek. All of us tacitly and unreflectively assume we have the capacity to know the world around us as it really is. Though we are aware that in any given case our conclusions might be wrong, we assume without much reflection that our interpretive faculties are reliable and give us a reliable understanding of reality (hence, Tacit *Realism*). Moreover, precisely because of this natural confidence in human perception, this kind of realism also tends to trust inherited cultural traditions. Tradition is questioned mainly when challenges are thrust upon it, as was the case when ancient Judeans were confronted by the fall of King David's "eternal" dynasty to Babylon (see Psalm 89).

Reflective Realism is the more philosophical twin of Tacit Realism. Its representatives included the likes of Plato and Aristotle as well as their later Christian interpreters Augustine and Aquinas. It too holds that human perception and tradition provide a generally trustworthy understanding of reality, but precisely because of its theoretical character, Reflective Realism explicates in more detail and subtlety both how and why traditions and perceptions can lead us astray. Here we might think of Plato's "Allegory of the Cave," wherein the shadows of things on a cave wall, cast by real things via firelight, might be easily confused with the things themselves.[2] Or we could consider the theological treatise of Aquinas, *Summa Theologica,* in which Father Thomas relentlessly interrogates

---

2. Plato, *The Republic,* tr. P. Shorey (2 vols.; LCL; Cambridge: Harvard University Press, 1942-43).

the Christian tradition with almost one hundred important questions, each explored in turn with still other questions and queries.[3] So, more than everyday Tacit Realism, Reflective Realists believe that we should think critically about our grasp of reality.

Reflective realism (which lives on today in some varieties of Thomistic philosophy) spawned intense examinations of humanity's epistemic condition and, in the process, generated that movement in philosophy commonly known as Modern Realism.

Modern Realism

This view emerged gradually during the course of the late Medieval, Renaissance (fourteenth and fifteenth centuries), Reformation (sixteenth century), and Enlightenment (seventeenth and eighteenth centuries) periods. Its origins and development are disputed at many points, but scholars generally agree that Modern Realism's roots were laid down as scholars in Europe (such as Petrarch and Ramus) rediscovered classical Greek and Roman traditions and judged these to be far more sophisticated than what was produced by medieval Christianity. At first, during the Renaissance, the result was rampant criticism of the medieval academic tradition, but this eventually developed into a critique of church tradition during the Reformation and then of the Bible itself during the Enlightenment.

Modern Realism is chiefly characterized by two related features. First, unlike everyday Tacit Realism and its more sophisticated twin Reflective Realism, Modern Realism is radically skeptical of tradition.[4] In fact, it regards tradition as a chief cause of human confusion and believes that we can only know "the truth" when we overcome human tradition by "rising above it," so to speak, in order to see the world "as it actually is." A second characteristic of Modern Realism is its epistemic optimism. It confidently believes that, by carefully interrogating and setting aside tradition, we can achieve an infallible, incorrigible, and indubitable grasp of the truth. As a

---

3. Thomas Aquinas, *Summa Theologica* (5 vols.; Allen, TX: Christian Classics, 1981).

4. Some modern philosophies are equally suspicious of perception and metaphysics, but here my emphasis is specifically on tradition.

result, on those points where we are very careful, we simply cannot be wrong. This epistemic posture (also known as *Strong Foundationalism*) is obviously very different from the stance of Premodern (Tacit and Reflective) Realism, in that these earlier approaches recognized that "certainty" did not guarantee knowledge.

As we move forward to the postmodern epistemologies, I would remind readers that Modern Realism is still alive and well on the contemporary epistemic scene.[5] It is especially prominent in everyday life and in some quarters of Christian Fundamentalism, where it supposedly guarantees the "assurance of salvation."[6] Paradoxically, the necessity for this theological move was engendered by Modernism itself, whose quest for indubitable, incorrigible certainty was adopted by Fundamentalists as the only appropriate basis for soteriological confidence.[7] As Lesslie Newbigin has pointed out, this was a serious mistake because human beings simply do not have access to incorrigible certainty in this or any matter.[8] Anxiety about salvation is often the result.

Postmodernism: Anti-Realism and Practical Realism

Though Modern Realism developed over a lengthy stretch of history, philosophy's love affair with it was rather short-lived. Philosophers living in the last days of philosophical Modernism — Kant, Hegel, Schopenhauer, Nietzsche, and Heidegger — gradually revealed that the epistemic project

5. The chief theoretical advocates in interpretation theory have been E. D. Hirsch, Jr., *Validity in Interpretation* (New Haven: Yale, 1967), and Emilio Betti, "Hermeneutics as the General Methodology of the *Geisteswissenschaften*," in *The Hermeneutic Tradition*, ed. G. Ormiston and A. Schrift (Albany, NY: SUNY Press, 1990), 159-97.

6. Examples include William Lane Craig and J. P. Moreland, *Philosophical Foundations for a Christian Worldview* (Downers Grove, IL: InterVarsity, 2003); Richard Lints, *The Fabric of Theology: A Prolegomenon to Evangelical Theology* (Grand Rapids: Eerdmans, 1993); and J. P. Moreland, "Truth, Contemporary Philosophy and the Postmodern Turn," *JETS* 48 (2005): 77-88.

7. See Merold Westphal, "Post-Kantian Reflections on the Importance of Hermeneutics," in *Disciplining Hermeneutics: Interpretation in Christian Perspective*, ed. R. Lundin (Grand Rapids: Eerdmans, 1997), 57-66.

8. Lesslie Newbigin, "Certainty as the Way to Nihilism," in *Proper Confidence: Faith, Doubt, and Certainty in Christian Discipleship* (Grand Rapids: Eerdmans, 1995), 29-44.

of Modern Realism was doomed all along to fail, for it aspired to the impossible goal of "escaping" tradition. All of us grow up in and are formed by culture and, because of this, inevitably begin our pursuit of the truth from *within* a cultural tradition. In our search for the truth, we simply cannot "start from scratch." We may swim with the current of tradition or against it, but tradition is always the water that we swim in. We are always wet and always pushed here and there by the current in ways that we do not realize.

Broadly speaking, this correct observation about the role of tradition in human life has yielded two schools of Postmodern epistemic thought.[9] One of these begins by agreeing with Modernism on this basic point: tradition *does* blind us to the truth. And if tradition inevitably shapes us and if it also blinds us to the truth, it follows that human beings simply do not know the truth: we do not know reality as it is. What we mistakenly embrace as "reality" is nothing other than *invention*, which is in turn a product of invented traditions. *Antirealism* and *Non-Realism* are among the names given to this view, which denies any connection between what we think about reality and reality itself.[10] The "truth" is *created* by human beings. Antirealists further hold that we do not create the world aimlessly but rather in exercises of power that enable us to control and exploit each other. As a result, many Antirealists involve themselves in ethical struggles to "deconstruct" the political and religious systems that oppress the powerless.[11]

Though I will not side theoretically with Antirealism, I would point out that Antirealists are certainly right about some things. Foremost, they recognize and try to combat the strong tendency in human beings to abuse power. Christian orthodoxy agrees with this and agrees, too, that we should make every effort to protect and care for the oppressed. Any-

9. P. M. Rosenau refers to these streams of thought as "skeptical" and "affirmative" postmodernism. See *Post-Modernism and the Social Sciences* (Princeton: Princeton University Press, 1992).

10. The best-known advocates of this view, alongside Nietzsche, would be Jacques Derrida, Michael Foucault, Jean-François Lyotard, and Richard Rorty (among others). For representative articles by each, see Kenneth Baynes, James Bohman, and Thomas McCarthy, eds., *After Philosophy: End or Transformation?* (Cambridge, MA: MIT Press, 1987).

11. For an introduction, see John D. Caputo, *Deconstruction in a Nutshell: A Conversation with Jacques Derrida* (New York: Fordham, 1997).

thing less is unchristian. Also accurate is the Antirealist observation that much of what passes as "true" in our world is invented. One only needs to consider that the English drive on the left and the Germans on the right to see that this so. This observation might seem mundane at first, but we should note that it is also true of religion. Just as cars drive on different sides of the road, so concepts of divinity and morality vary widely from culture to culture. Thus, the important theoretical question is *not* whether humans invent or construct our views of reality. We do. The pertinent question is whether these invented strategies for getting along in the world are *mere* invention (as Antirealists claim) or whether, in fact, they rightly reflect something true about the world we live in and about the people with whom we share this world.

I am personally much more comfortable with the other Postmodern response to Modernism. This approach — which I have already introduced as *Practical Realism* — charts a course between the epistemic optimism of Modern Realism and the pessimism of Antirealism, but it does not get there by simple moderation, as if one had mixed hot and cold water to get something lukewarm. It begins by strongly disagreeing with Modern Realism and Antirealism at the very points where those two errant views agree. Modern Realism and Antirealism agree that (1) knowledge only counts if you can demonstrate that it is incorrigibly certain, and (2) that human tradition blinds us to the truth. The two epistemologies disagree only on whether tradition is something that we can overcome. Antirealism claims that we cannot overcome tradition and hence we cannot see "reality," whereas Modern Realism believes that we can overcome tradition and hence are able to grasp reality.

By way of contrast, Practical Realism offers these claims:[12] First, it

12. In spite of *significant* differences among them, chief advocates of practical realism include the likes of Donald Davidson, Hans-Georg Gadamer, Jürgen Habermas, Alasdair MacIntyre, Michael Polanyi, Paul Ricoeur, Charles Taylor, Merold Westphal, and Ludwig Wittgenstein, among others. For representative essays by most of these scholars, see Baynes, Bohman, and McCarthy, *After Philosophy*. For Polanyi, Westphal, and Wittgenstein, see Michael Polanyi, *Personal Knowledge: Towards a Post-Critical Philosophy* (London: Routledge, 1998); Merold Westphal, *Whose Community? Which Interpretation?* (Grand Rapids: Baker, 2009); and Ludwig Wittgenstein, *Philosophical Investigations*, tr. G. E. M. Anscombe (Oxford: Blackwell. 1953).

avers that we need not prove that we are right in order to have genuine knowledge. This is why young children, who have no epistemic theories at all, can have knowledge without proving it to themselves or others.[13] And second, Practical Realism does not believe that cultural traditions blind us to the truth; rather, it believes that *tradition is the very way that human beings grasp the truth*. Tradition is *right* about the world (generally speaking) because, by its nature, tradition is the product of humanity's successful engagement with a real world and real people, "the democracy of the dead."[14] So we can and should trust tradition. This is true of the Christian tradition itself and also of cultural traditions in general. The fact that some cultural traditions might be "better" or "healthier" than others does not gainsay this basic point.

On the other hand, Practical Realism agrees that Modern Realism and Antirealism are *partly* right when they are suspicious of tradition, since tradition is always warped and always wrong in some ways or others. In spite of our very best efforts to avoid mistakes, what we have to say about things like business, economics, literature, philosophy, psychology, and history always errs to some extent, and this goes double for something like theology, where our goal is to describe God and his dealings with humanity. Nevertheless, even respecting these matters, Practical Realism believes that tradition can provide a useful and adequate grasp on the reality. The grasp is not on a toggle switch that is either right or wrong. Rather, it lies on a continuum between better and poorer: it can be very good or very bad, but never perfect. In the best cases, human knowledge is *wholly adequate* for the needs of our situation.

But what, precisely, is the nature of this "adequate" correlation between interpretation and fact? Unlike Modern Realism, which posits an actual one-for-one correspondence between interpretation and fact, Practical Realism accounts for interpretive success in terms of analogy and metaphor.[15] For instance, in a satisfying conversation with a friend about

13. This view of epistemology is called "externalism." The contrary position, which demands that knowledge must be based on self-conscious interrogation, is called "internalism."

14. G. K. Chesterton, *Orthodoxy* (Wheaton, IL: Harold Shaw, 1994), 47.

15. In a sense, Practical Realism merely extends the analogical theology of Aquinas (that we must speak of divinity analogically and not univocally) to our talk about the cre-

my feelings and thoughts, the result will *not* be that my friend has at any point actually understood my thoughts and feelings as I understand them. Rather, my friend's understanding will be similar or analogous to what I have tried to express, so that I feel understood in some way or other. We could pragmatically call the conversation "perfect" in the loose and practical sense (in that it accomplished my desired objectives), but it would not be an instance of error-free interpretation. For my friend undoubtedly errs in some ways as he tries to understand me, and, to make the issues clearer, I will undoubtedly err in understanding myself.

How is "Practical Realism," as construed here, any different from the "pragmatic" epistemology of an antirealist like Richard Rorty? Rorty would agree with just about everything I have said, that we always engage the world with a sense of "getting it right," that we move forward pragmatically in an effort to understand, that we work to advance toward our human goals and aspirations. So again, what is the difference?

Rorty holds that there is no relationship between the interpretation of something (such as a text) and the "truth" about it. As he expressed it, "we do not need a goal called 'truth' . . . any more than our digestive organs need a goal called 'health' to set them to work."[16] Rorty seems to hold this view for two reasons. On the one hand, he believes that there is no way to prove that we have our facts right and, hence, we cannot really claim to know the "Truth." On the other hand, and perhaps more importantly, Rorty offers a theological assertion: "there would only be a 'higher' aim of inquiry called 'truth' if there were such a thing as *ultimate* justification — justification before God, or before the tribunal of reason, as opposed to any merely finite human audience."[17] Thus, Rorty believes that, apart from some final arbiter of the "truth," there is simply no such thing as the truth.

---

ated order in general. For a discussion that also highlights the Christological limits of analogy for Aquinas, see Bruce D. Marshall, "Christ the End of Analogy," in *The Analogy of Being: Invention of the Antichrist or Wisdom of God?* ed. T. J. White (Grand Rapids: Eerdmans, 2011), 280-313.

16. Richard Rorty, *Philosophy and Social Hope* (New York: Penguin, 1999), 37-38. For a discussion that interprets Rorty through the lens of practical realism, see R. J. Snell, *Through a Glass Darkly: Bernard Lonergan and Richard Rorty on Knowing without a God's-Eye View* (Milwaukee: Marquette University Press, 2006).

17. Rorty, *Philosophy and Social Hope*, 38.

Contrary to Rorty's pragmatism, Practical Realists believe that the phenomenon or experience of "getting things right" is a meaningful epistemic clue. Though we cannot *prove* that our interpretations are getting the world "right," the ubiquitous sense of "getting it right" suggests that this is precisely what is happening. While Rorty holds fast to the modernist demand for indubitable "proof" before he will admit to know something "true" about the "real" world, Practical Realists believe that the evidence better suits a Realist epistemology. That is, we may safely infer that our interpretations are getting *something right* about the world and about the human beings who live in it. As for Rorty's comment about God and truth, from a Christian standpoint his argument is moot: God *will* convene an ultimate tribunal on the truth, so our pursuit of the truth, and our successful grasp of it, makes a great deal of difference.

In the final analysis, the fundamental differences among Modernism, Antirealism, and Practical Realism can be expressed with the commonly used metaphor of "capital T" versus "small t" truth. Modernists believe that human beings can attain the "Truth," Antirealists maintain that "Truth" does not exist, and Practical Realists believe that "the Truth," though it exists, is accessible to human beings only by analogies that yield partial, useful, "small t" truths. As Merold Westphal expressed it, "the truth is that there is Truth, but not for us, only for God."[18] As I have suggested already, I believe that the practical, analogical approach is far superior to the others.

I would mention in passing that recent work in cognitive psychology has yielded a broad consensus that human cognition is driven by "small t" analogies and metaphors.[19] Successful interpretations do not involve mirror images of the world so much as noetic models that correlate to the world and allow us to get along within it. The debate is no longer whether, but how, this analogical apparatus serves our interpretive activities. So Practical Realism and cognitive psychology, while working from different

18. Merold Westphal, *Overcoming Onto-Theology: Toward a Postmodern Christian Faith* (New York: Fordham University Press, 2001), ix. See also John R. Franke, *Manifold Witness: The Plurality of Truth* (Nashville: Abingdon, 2009), 11-19.

19. See the collection of essays in Dedre Gentner, Keith J. Holyak, and Boicho N. Kokinov, eds., *The Analogical Mind: Perspectives from Cognitive Science* (Cambridge, MA: MIT Press, 2001).

sets of data and using very different modes of engagement, are arriving at the same theoretical destination.

Lest there be confusion on this point, I want to accentuate before moving ahead that Practical Realism *does* believe that there are such things as "right" and "wrong," "correct" and "incorrect," "certainty" and "uncertainty," "knowledge" and "ignorance." But these words have different nuances for Practical Realists than for Modern Realists. "Knowledge" means that we have an understanding of the world that is analogous to, but not identical with, the realities that we seek to understand. "Correct" means that our judgment yields practical success rather than precise and perfect understanding. As for "certainty," Practical Realists regard this as the *perception* that "We *must* be right."[20] The trick is that, while this perception is absolutely essential for our everyday hermeneutical engagements and generally serves us well in the practical sense, in the final analysis it does not yield capital T "Truth" or guarantee that we are right. We can be both quite certain and quite wrong. *C'est la vie.*

Practical Realism offers numerous advantages over the alternative theories. Though it is the product of a long and sophisticated dialogue about epistemology and is advocated by many trained philosophers, it stands surprisingly close to the Tacit Realism that dominates the everyday life of people who are not professional theologians and philosophers. Tacit Realism and Practical Realism both recognize that we get some things right and some things wrong, and that a sense of certainty does not guarantee epistemic success. Any good epistemic theory should dovetail fairly well with Tacit Realism, and Practical Realism does just that.

Tacit Knowledge, Tradition, and Experience

We have said that tradition plays a fundamental role in human understanding. Thanks to the work of Michael Polanyi, we can say something more about how tradition plays this role.[21] Polanyi points out that human

20. For this description of certainty, see John Henry Newman, *A Grammar of Assent* (Garden City, NY: Doubleday, 1955), 135-208.
21. Michael Polanyi, *The Tacit Dimension* (Gloucester, MA: Peter Smith, 1983).

82

knowledge always runs deeper than words can say. For example, we can recognize someone's face, or infer emotion from one's facial expressions, without being able to say precisely what the indicators are. Polanyi describes this rich, full-bodied knowledge as "tacit knowledge." An important consequence of his insight is that, whenever we make explicit knowledge claims or engage in substantive discussions and debates, our discourse always depends on a deeper knowledge which, by virtue of its complexity and depth, is beyond our ability to describe. So there is no such thing as a conversation, or speech, or article, or book that wholly "gets at" what we understand (or think we understand) about a given subject. Many debates and arguments are intractable precisely because they stem from fundamental differences of opinion and interpretation that are deep and tacit, of the sort that cannot easily be put into words.

Whence comes this "tacit dimension" of human knowledge? In many respects, tradition determines the shape and texture of our rich but ineffable grasp on everyday life. I refer here to tradition in its broadest sense, in terms of our national and cultural context, and also in its more narrow sense, in terms of our immediate family and community. But tacit knowledge is also shaped by personal experiences, and it is here that it is shown to be both the preserver and the interrogator of tradition. It preserves tradition by its tendency to casually embrace and be shaped by tradition, but it interrogates tradition when personal experience seems to counter and contradict traditional assumptions. Among other things, this reminds us that each individual's experience is unique and will, if we attend to it, add a distinctive perspective to our total portrait of the human situation.[22]

Incidentally, the tacit dimension of human knowledge has important implications for our construal of textual interpretation. Peter Leithart has pointed out that reading a text, such as the Bible, is a bit like getting a joke: you only get it if you have the right combination of information, imagination, and insight to grasp the subtle point that is being made.[23]

---

22. Here I would point readers to the work of Emmanuel Levinas, who accentuates the primacy of tacit experience in human relationships and the ethical importance of taking every human individual seriously. For an entry into his work, see Emmanuel Levinas, *The Levinas Reader*, ed. Seán Hand (Oxford: Blackwell, 1989).

23. Peter J. Leithart, *Deep Exegesis: The Mystery of Reading Scripture* (Waco: Baylor University Press, 2009), 109-39.

So good biblical interpretation depends on tacit insight. It is art more than science.

Polanyi's observations are elegantly simple and very important. I will return to them later on in our discussion.

Culture and Reason

Much more could be said about Practical Realism, but in the interest of economy I would like to touch at this point on only two closely related subjects, *culture* and *reason*. Postmodernism challenges the modern perception that cultures are discrete, closed systems with clear boundaries that separate one culture from another.[24] Cultures are in fact overlapping social modalities and networks with porous boundaries that are always in flux and to some degree or other matters of contention. As an example, in my own case, I would say that I have some semblance of identity within the following cultural sets and subsets: in Christianity (evangelical, Anglican, and ecumenical), in biblical scholarship (secular and confessional circles), and in various "local" American identities (suburban, rural Appalachia, cosmopolitan Northeast, and deep South). My identity, like the identities of most people in the world, is more complex than first meets the eye.

One implication of the foregoing is that individual members of a social modality — such as a culture or religious tradition — do not share identical ideas and viewpoints. Shared beliefs and opinions are actually analogies with overlapping concepts and perceptions. Real differences are therefore inevitable and lead inexorably to the internal conflicts and disagreements that arise in human institutions and traditions. This reminds us that cultural identities fit neatly within Practical Realism's larger paradigm of human epistemology, according to which our grasp of reality is by analogy rather than by full correspondence between perception and fact. I mention this especially to point out that these cultural limits are true, not only of me and you, but also of those who wrote the Bible. A case in point appears in

24. See Kevin J. Vanhoozer, *The Drama of Doctrine: A Canonical-Linguistic Approach to Christian Theology* (Louisville: Westminster John Knox Press, 2005), 121; Sheila Geeve Davaney, "Theology and the Turn to Cultural Analysis," in *Converging on Culture: Theologians in Dialogue with Cultural Analysis and Criticism* (Oxford: Oxford University Press, 2001), 3-16.

1 Cor 11:14-15, where the Apostle Paul incorrectly assumes that "nature it-self" proves that men should have short hair and women long hair. He did not realize that this inference was drawn through a cultural lens rather than directly from the natural order. Errors of this sort are endemic to human judgment. Try as we may, we simply cannot avoid them.

Turning to the subject of "reason," I begin with this observation. While the old Modernism imagined that human reason was the same in every person, Postmodernists do not believe anything like this. According to Postmodernism, rationality is culturally shaped and differs from culture to culture and, to some extent, even from person to person. To be sure, there are similarities between American, Brazilian, Nigerian, Christian, and Hindu "rationalities," in that members of these cultural modalities share analogous capacities and use comparable strategies to organize and order their thoughts about the world in a coherent way. But when it comes to how we order and understand things like morals, ethics, history, politics, and religion — things human and divine — there are differences, sometimes dramatic differences. Practical Realism would also resist modern conceptions of reason that haphazardly pit it against things like emotions and intuition. Rationality is better construed as a noetic capacity that involves not only the cognitive (intellectual) but also the affective (emotional) and conative (volitional/decision-making) dimensions of the mind. Some scholars believe that, in matters of moral judgment, emotion actually plays a more prominent role than abstract reasoning.[25]

But, these limitations accepted and acknowledged, when it comes to interpretation, *reason* (in the robust noetic sense) remains a fundamental element of the hermeneutical game. To "understand," "read," "explain," or "decide" is always an exercise in which we take various elements — facts, words, objects, ideas, concepts, feelings, intuitions, what have you — and try to rightly relate them in a coherent way. So we must use our reason to live life and to do theology. Practical Realism optimistically believes that our culturally conditioned rationalities have the capacity to help us make sense of our world and our experiences in it.

25. Jonathan Haidt, "The Emotional Dog and Its Rational Tail: A Social Intuitionist Approach to Moral Judgment," *Psychological Review* 108 (2001), 814-34; Cordelia Fine, "Is the Emotional Dog Wagging Its Rational Tail, or Chasing It?" *Philosophical Explorations* 9 (2006), 83-98.

Practical Realism and Christian Faith

Biblical interpretation has stood in the foreground or background of hermeneutical discussions for a long time, so there is already an implicit connection between the foregoing discussion and the concerns of faith. Here I will make the connection more explicit.

If Practical Realism is a good description of how human beings actually conduct our lives, then we can anticipate that its basic contours are implied in many sources and places, including in biblical thought. And this is indeed the case. The Bible is introduced by an epistemic commentary. I refer to the Fall of humanity in Genesis, which the biblical author traces back to humanity's errant pursuit of divine knowledge (Genesis 3).[26] Whatever insight the first couple gained from that pursuit (they became "like God, knowing good and evil"), the result was not suited to them, nor did it entail all divine knowledge. So as we begin to read Scripture, it immediately steers us away from the idea that human beings can or should see the world as God sees it.

The author of the book of Job provides a fuller explication of this principle by deftly sketching out the profound contrast between divine and human knowledge.[27] Job's pious friends believed that his suffering (in fact, all suffering) was a consequence of sin, whereas Job claimed to be an innocent sufferer. As the story unfolds we learn that Job's theology is "right" and that his friends were "wrong." Righteous people do suffer. But the author's epistemic point runs much deeper, I think. For it is quite clear that *Job was right only in comparison with his friends.* When finally Job's wisdom was placed alongside God's, we see something different. As God expressed it, "Will you [Job] question me, mere mortal? . . . Where were you when I created the cosmos?"[28] Job quickly repented in response, admit-

---

26. See Cardinal Joseph Ratzinger, *In the Beginning: A Catholic Understanding of the Story of Creation and the Fall* (Grand Rapids: Eerdmans, 1995), 64-71; Gerhard von Rad, *Genesis: A Commentary* (rev ed.; Philadelphia: Westminster Press, 1973), 86-90.

27. For discussion, see Ryan P. O'Dowd, "A Chord of Three Strands: Epistemology in Job, Proverbs and Ecclesiastes," in *The Bible and Epistemology: Biblical Soundings on the Knowledge of God*, ed. M. Healy and R. Parry (Milton Keynes, UK: Paternoster, 2007), 65-87.

28. A paraphrastic summary of Job 38–41.

ting sheepishly that he had uttered "what I did not understand, things too wonderful for me, which I did not know" (Job 42:3).

In practical terms it is perfectly suitable to say that Job was right and his friends were wrong, but on closer inspection we easily see that this description of the situation is convenient shorthand. We would more precisely say that Job and his friends were *partly right* and *partly wrong*, but in a way that made Job's partial understanding of human suffering more complete and healthy than that of his friends. But in the end even Job repented, for in this biblical story about epistemology, only God gets everything right.

Does this staid and humble view of human knowledge appear in the New Testament as well? Yes, I believe that it does. Paul accentuates the difference between human and divine knowledge when he describes God's wisdom and judgments as "unsearchable" and "inscrutable" (Rom 11:33-36). Paul's comments to the Corinthians also come immediately to mind: "My conscience is clear, but that does not make me innocent. It is the Lord who judges me," and "Now we see in a mirror dimly" (1 Cor 4:3-4; 13:12). The apostle was fully aware that human perspectives are neither god-like nor foolproof. So, although Paul refers elsewhere in 1 Corinthians to the special spiritual insights available to Christians (2:6-16), he seems to have understood that this special knowledge of the Spirit, whatever it entails, does not guarantee that we will get things right. To demand more is merely to repeat the sins of our first parents, who ate from a tree in pursuit of divine knowledge. At best we find ourselves in Job's epistemic position. That is, *perhaps* we have a better understanding of things than someone else, but we never have it spot-on and, if pressed, must repent in dust and ashes. This is Christian Practical Realism in a nutshell: God has it perfectly right, while human beings are partially right and partially wrong, but in a way that admits some human perspectives are better or more adequate than others.

I shall add one more point before concluding this chapter. If finite human beings get things wrong in the nature of the case, then our epistemic capacities are doubly limited if human beings are fallen creatures, as the Christian tradition says we are. Whether consciously or unconsciously, human interpretation twists and contorts the evidence to suit our vices. The epistemic effect of sin is so obvious that some philosophers, who pro-

SACRED WORD, BROKEN WORD

fess to have no theological interests at all, will nevertheless admit that there is something "fallen" about our human interpretations of the world.[29] According to Scripture, unless we admit that we are blind in this way, we will not be able to "see" (John 9:41).

Is it a happy coincidence that Practical Realism is compatible with a biblically and theologically informed description of the human situation? I do not believe so. Practical Realism developed out of philosophical discussions engendered and shaped by the Christian tradition itself.[30] H.-G. Gadamer, in many respects the forefather of Practical Realism, freely confessed the role of Augustine in his thinking. It would be a mistake, then, to assume that Christian advocates of Practical Realism such as myself are merely seeking to baptize a philosophy that appeals to us. The relationship between Practical Realism and Christianity is organic.

Given that Practical Realism is an adequately Christian description of human knowledge and discourse, we should not be at all surprised to find (as we have) that Scripture, as a book written by fallible human beings, is itself a book of theological discourse that advances the truth but also stands in need of redemption. Scripture is beautiful *and* broken, and it is being read and studied in the church, and sometimes outside of the church, by beautiful and broken human beings. Nevertheless, Christians have theological and philosophical reasons to suppose that, when we read Scripture well, we are able to understand it. And as we understand it, we shall find that God's truth and beauty run deeper, and are more potent, than the brokenness that God is healing.

---

29. Heidegger and Derrida, for example. See James K. A. Smith, *The Fall of Interpretation: Philosophical Foundations for a Creational Hermeneutics* (Downers Grove: InterVarsity, 2000), 104-21.

30. Regarding this point, see Jens Zimmerman, *Recovering Theological Hermeneutics: An Incarnational-Trinitarian Theory of Interpretation* (Grand Rapids: Baker, 2004).

CHAPTER 9

Sacred Scripture as Ancient Discourse

There is a difference between reading the Bible and reading Holy Scripture. Anyone can read the Bible, including those who debunk or detest it. But to read the Bible as *Holy Scripture* is to embrace it as authoritative discourse from God, as a book in which God directs us toward abundant life in Jesus Christ. In the next few chapters I will sketch out an approach for reading the Bible as Holy Scripture. My approach stands generally within an emerging contemporary movement that goes by names like "theological interpretation" or "theological hermeneutics." The movement is characterized by its *creedal, ecumenical, biblical* and *theological* character.

Theological interpretation is creedal because its participants embrace the Christian tradition and its great statements of theological orthodoxy, such as the Nicene Creed and Definition of Chalcedon, as foundational for biblical interpretation. The movement is ecumenical because it acknowledges that creedal boundaries leave room for a wide variety of legitimate faith expressions and commitments. Scholars from Catholic, Protestant, and Eastern Orthodox communities, some more conservative and others more liberal, are all welcomed to the table of discussion and debate. The movement is biblical because its participants take Scripture seriously and believe that a thoughtful, informed engagement with the Bible is essential for the health of the church. Many players in theological interpretation come from traditions where this has not always been the case, so in some respects we may speak here about the "rediscovery" of Scripture. Finally, as its name implies, the movement is "theological" as opposed to merely "biblical." Theological interpreters are committed to the Chalcedonian principle that Scripture is both divine and human and that, because of this, it teaches theology through the limited perspectives of the human horizon. This implies that Scripture is theologically diverse and that each biblical text contributes a distinctive voice to our theological reflection. As a result, nearly every modern book written in the genre of "theological interpretation" will refer to the inevitable "struggle" that theological interpretation entails. One cannot simply read theology off of the Bible's pages; one must understand the text and then reflect theologically on what is said in light of other biblical texts and in light of God's voice as it speaks to us through tradition, cosmos, experience, and Spirit.

My approach differs from the movement's general trend on at least one basic point. I believe that we should engage Scripture by reading it as an ancient book and by trying to understand what its ancient writers wished to say.[1] In recent years, theological interpretation has moved away from this approach. The human authors of Scripture are often set to one side (more or less) so that greater emphasis can be laid on hearing the words of the Bible's divine author. In extreme cases, theological interpreters actually ignore the Bible's human discourse because they find it problematic or offensive. While I have *some* sympathy with this approach (as I will eventually explain), I do not share it fully and will discuss later on why, in my opinion, theology has tended to move in this direction.

Scripture as Ancient Human Discourse

God provided Scripture through words written by ancient authors who lived in diverse social and historical contexts. It seems to me that we best

1. For several arguments in favor of the Bible's human authors, see John Barton, *The Nature of Biblical Criticism* (Louisville: Westminster John Knox, 2007); Joseph A. Fitzmyer, *The Interpretation of Scripture: In Defense of the Historical-Critical Method* (New York: Paulist Press, 2008); Peter J. Leithart, *Deep Exegesis: The Mystery of Reading Scripture* (Waco: Baylor University Press, 2009); Kevin J. Vanhoozer, *Is There a Meaning in This Text? The Bible, The Reader, and the Morality of Literary Knowledge* (Grand Rapids: Zondervan, 1998); Francis Watson, *Text and Truth: Redefining Biblical Theology* (Edinburgh: T. & T. Clark, 1997).

honor this design by treating the Bible as the ancient text that it is. So if we want to read the Epistle to Romans well, we will *try* to receive it as Paul's words and, in doing so, inform ourselves about the historical situation and context of Paul's day insofar as this is feasible. In a sense, God speaks to us in Romans as we "listen in" on what he once said through Paul to first-century Christians in Rome. So, as Augustine pointed out long ago, a healthy approach to Scripture takes seriously the significant historical and cultural gap that separates the original discourse from its later readers.[2]

We need not sketch a detailed agenda for the contextually and historically sensitive interpretation of Scripture. Many scholars have already done this. The basic point is simply that we are in a better position to understand the biblical text when we know something about its author and the world in which he lived and wrote. If there is a particular point to emphasize, it would be that our attention to the historical and contextual contingency of Scripture should include sensitivity to the literary genres of Scripture. That is, we will try to avoid repeating the infamous mistake of Archbishop Ussher (1581-1656), who mistook the Bible for a very precise historical document and on that basis errantly calculated that God created the cosmos on October 22, 4004 BCE.[3] The universe is, of course, much older, and it is now widely recognized that much of the biblical "chronology" was never intended as an accurate rendering of conventional history.[4] In this case and many others, careful attention to the ancient context of the Bible, and especially to the kinds of literature it contains, helps us understand the text better and reveals that some of the Bible's "problems" are not problems at all.

The Bible contains a dizzying array of genres: histories, myths, novellas, tales, parables, legends, biographies, autobiographies, letters, genealogies, king lists, itineraries, theophanies, rituals, treaties, prophecies, apocalypses, proverbs, laments, love poetry, songs, and even a work of

2. *On Christian Doctrine* 2.42 (NPNF1 2.549).
3. James Barr, "Why the World Was Created in 4004 B.C.: Archbishop Ussher and Biblical Chronology," *Bulletin of the John Rylands Library* 67 (1985): 575-608.
4. See Kenton L. Sparks, *Ancient Texts for the Study of the Hebrew Bible: A Guide to the Background Literature* (Peabody: Hendrickson, 2005), 344-60. For a classic conservative attempt to address this problem, see William Henry Green, "Primeval Chronology: Are There Gaps in the Biblical Genealogies?" *BibSac* 47 (1890): 285-303.

philosophical skepticism (Ecclesiastes). None of the biblical books correspond precisely to any genres of modern literature. So if we approach a book like Genesis as if it were modern science, the Joseph novella as history, John's Gospel as mere biography, Paul's letters as philosophy, or the apocalypses like Daniel and Revelation as books of prophecy, the results can be very misleading and confusing. In many cases the content of the books is closer to "folk wisdom" than to the "philosophical wisdom" we find in the writings of Plato and Aristotle. This is certainly true of Proverbs and of the primitive science and anthropology in Genesis 1–11, but even Paul's letters — often considered among the most theological in the Bible — had to be defended against the charge that they were intellectually and rhetorically inferior to Greco-Roman scholarship.[5] I do not say this to disparage the Bible. Rather, I mean to resist philosophical elitism by claiming that everyday human discourse has the capacity to bear serious and enlightening theological truth. The Bible is a collection of texts written using ancient literary models by authors steeped in the pragmatic concerns of everyday life in an ancient world. We should read it as such.

To be sure, if we apply this contextually and generically sensitive approach to a study of Paul's letter to the Romans, this will not guarantee a good grasp of his message. We might badly miss the sense of Paul's letter. Even in the best scenario our understanding will not wholly grasp it and will even misunderstand it in some way or other. But as is the case when we read our mail or speak with others face to face, we have the best chance of successfully understanding the Bible's authors when we make an effort to listen to them. That is, the best way to read Romans is to *try to listen* to Paul. As I have said already, such an approach honors God's design, which was to speak to ancient audiences through the words of particular contextually-situated human beings.

An assumption commonly made in historical, contextually-sensitive readings of Scripture is that our goal is to understand the "intentions" of the author. While the sentiment is well-placed, a bit of reflection reveals an underlying complexity. For often enough attending to an author's in-

---

5. Paul's intellect and literary style are defended in the 4th-century pseudepigraphic "Correspondence of Paul and Seneca." See J. K. Elliott, *The Apocryphal New Testament* (Oxford: Clarendon, 1993), 547-554.

tentions will paradoxically lead us away from them. This is most obvious when the text is a work of art that inspires aesthetic experiences rather than cognition (certain kinds of poetry, for example), but the same is true of other texts. When Luke wrote his Gospel, for instance, he did not necessarily imagine that readers would pursue his "intentions." Rather, he hoped that they would understand the story of Jesus and respond in an appropriate way. Authors certainly "mean something" with the text, and readers certainly assume that texts were written by authorial agents with intentions and aims. But again, a *pursuit* of those intentions was not necessarily the author's goal. In fact, authors sometimes try to conceal or veil their underlying intentions.

I suspect, nonetheless, that reading almost always involves the author's intention in some way, not merely as the assumed background but as something we really want to understand. This is very natural when the author has specifically cited his aims in the text, as the author of 1 John did in his letter: "I am writing this to you so that you may not sin" (2:1). Authorial intention also comes to the fore when we are confused by the Bible's discourse. When Augustine attempted to make sense of the confusing genealogies in Genesis, for example, he inquired about the intentions of "he who wrote this record."[6] This, too, is a very natural response to the text and reveals the close, underlying connection between textual meaning and authorial aim. Authorial intention is also important when we critically reflect on the Bible. I am not referring here to "historical criticism" but to the more basic way in which we reflect critically on how to respond to an author's text. When we recognize that Luke has "challenged" us to respond to Jesus Christ or that Amos has "demanded" that we care for the poor, we have moved behind the inferred meaning of the text to an inference about the author's intentions. Successful readers realize what the authors want us to do — what they intended by their texts.

The more critically we reflect on the text, the more salient the author's intentions and aims become. For example, biblical scholars — who tend to be very critical — are not satisfied with a catalogue of the differences among the four Gospels. They also want to know *why* they are different. Inevitably, this line of inquiry raises other questions about the particular

6. *City of God* 15.20 (NPNF1 2.300).

aims of each Evangelist. Many scholarly judgments are based on an assessment of authorial intention. Scholars believe the author of Deuteronomy intended to supplant Assyrian power, that the author of 2 Kings intended to explain the causes of the exile, that Daniel and Revelation were intended to encourage suffering believers, and that the story of David was intended to defend his claim to the throne. When we understand these underlying intentions, we are better able to understand the meaning and significance of biblical discourse for its original audience and for us.

In Defense of the Human Author

As I have indicated, my emphasis on the Bible's human authors is out of step with current trends in theological hermeneutics. Some scholars do not believe that an ancient author's message and aims can be deduced from a written text, and others, though allowing this in principle, believe that the Bible is so distant culturally and historically that it is practically impossible to figure out what its authors "meant." As evidence for this latter point, theorists often point out that biblical scholars, who purport to use the same historical and contextual methods for reading the Bible, arrive at different and often contradictory interpretations of "the author's intention."[7] The same theorists often point out that we simply cannot recover the "intentions" of long-dead authors. As alternatives, these scholars usually advance "text-centered" or "reader-response" approaches. The first assumes that meaning lies *in* the text, while the second assumes that readers *create* meaning as they interact with the text. Neither scenario attends closely to the concerns of the text's original human author.

I do not agree with this assessment of our situation. First, scholars who pessimistically criticize the mixed results of biblical scholarship disagree themselves about how to proceed once they have jettisoned the author's intentions. So the meaning of Scripture is contested by everyone — not only by those who pursue the author's aims but also by those who do not. Secondly, disagreements about the author's message and intention

---

7. A. K. M. Adam, *Faithful Interpretation: Reading the Bible in a Postmodern World* (Minneapolis: Fortress, 2006), 92.

are not evidence that ancient authors cannot be understood. These disagreements merely remind us that some interpretations get at the author's message better than others. The fact that we cannot prove but can only judge which interpretation is better has no bearing on this fact. Third, the human author's "intention" takes pride of place in long-standing Christian tradition. Even in Christian antiquity, where allegory was widely used, the church fathers assumed that readers of Scripture should pursue "the intention of the author through whom the Holy Spirit spoke."[8] There was no need to defend Scripture's natural or literal sense but only its allegorical sense. And whenever the fathers found allegories in the Bible, they generally believed that the allegories were intended by the Bible's human authors because they quite naturally assumed that Scripture was human discourse that reflected the aims and concerns of inspired human authors.

Author-focused interpretation is receiving new support from modern neuroscience. Specialists have demonstrated that human beings do indeed try to "read the minds" of others, that is, to infer from their words, movements, and expressions what they are thinking and intending.[9] The human brain is characterized by an evolutionary hypertrophy (enlargement) in those areas that help us interpret other people by postulating and inferring their beliefs, perceptions, desires, knowledge, and inner states, among other things.[10] Scientists refer to this as a "theory of the mind," in

8. Here and elsewhere, language of authorial "intention" permeates Augustine's discussion of biblical interpretation. See *On Christian Doctrine* 3.10, 12 (NPNF1 2.560-62). It is commonly suggested that in antiquity Christian interpreters allowed for many levels or kinds of meaning, especially allegorical meanings. While this is certainly true, there can be no doubt that authorial intention — in terms of the human and divine authors of Scripture — has enjoyed the highest priority. This is why those who used allegory extensively (such as Augustine) found it necessary to defend allegory, as did those who used it more sparingly (such as Aquinas). Furthermore, we should not overlook the fact that many Christians, from antiquity to the present, have been very uncomfortable with "spiritual meanings" of the text. I have in mind the Antiochene Fathers like Theodore of Mopsuestia and Theodoret of Cyrrhus, medieval scholars like Nicholas of Lyra, Reformation scholars like Calvin and Luther, and a host of modern biblical scholars and theologians.

9. Malcolm Jeeves and Warren S. Brown, *Neuroscience, Psychology, and Religion: Illusions, Delusion, and Realities about Human Nature* (West Conshohocken, PA: Templeton Foundation Press, 2009), 54-90.

10. Pascal Boyer, "Functional Origins of Religious Concepts: Ontological and Strategic

the sense that we relate to other people by tacitly formulating "theories" about what they are thinking. Whether we do this successfully depends on lots of things, but *that* we are trying to do it, and *that* we tolerably succeed in many cases, can no longer be questioned.

As in face-to-face contexts, we interpret the Bible's written discourse by drawing inferences about what its authors were trying to say. The written word does not bear these meanings but rather is the vital *clue* by which we infer meaning. To get the sense of the discourse, we must imagine a context, in terms of the thoughts and intentions of authors and audiences, that will make the written text sensible. If we neglect this contextual step, we will simply read the text as if it were written directly to us and our modern situation. Whether confusion or harm is caused by this oversight depends on the text in question and the contextual particulars of the ancient and modern situation. As a rule, the closer our modern assumptions are to the ancient situation, the less we will misunderstand or be confused by the ancient discourse.

But that said, it remains the case that careful interpretation does not guarantee success. Even our best readings fall well short of full correspondence, yielding useful analogies that adequately seize on what the authors were trying to convey. Theorists highlight the "distance" between readers and authors by distinguishing the actual authors of ancient texts from the so-called *implied authors* that we, as later readers, imaginatively reconstruct. We can likewise note the difference between the real and implied audiences of ancient texts (for example, the difference between Paul's Roman audience and the Roman audience that we imagine as readers). The two things — real and implied — are *never* precisely the same and may be very different.

What should we do if we can make no sense of the biblical author's discourse? The best response is to honestly confess our confusion and continue our study until something sensible and convincing emerges. By all means, I do not think that we should build our theology on "the text" or on its "divine meaning" if we do not have a good sense of what its human author was getting at. There are parts of Scripture that we simply do not understand very well.

Selection in Evolved Minds," *Journal of the Royal Anthropology Institute* 6 (2000): 195-214, especially 203.

The Complexity and Limitations of Authorial Intention

The distinction between real and implied authors reminds us that authorial intention does not provide a "determinate meaning" that controls the results of interpretation. Meanings are pursued and inferred, but we cannot deduce them perfectly and could easily miss them badly. So I disagree with those theorists who believe that authorial intention provides a stable "boundary" for interpretation.[11] We are better off to say that the author's meaning provides *one* important *goal* of interpretation. On the road of textual interpretation the guardrails are few. Good readers try to stay on the road.

The road has many twists and turns. One of the twists is that human beings do not engage in written communication with a single intention but rather with multiple and sometimes competing motives and aims. When the apostle Paul referred to his need for financial support, as he did in almost all of his letters, did he do so with one intention? He told the Philippians that he broached the subject merely to teach the spiritual benefits of giving (Phil 4:17), but surely he hoped to secure more support, as he spells out elsewhere (Rom 15:24). The fact that he does not quite spell this out in every case does not prevent us from deciding that garnering financial support really was one of his intentions. When it comes to motives and meanings, we should expect that the natural ambiguities and complexities behind everyday discourse also stood behind the discourse of the biblical authors.

Another twist in the road: though we may assume general consistency in the writings and thoughts of ancient authors, we should not presume utter consistency in their thoughts and ideas. Consider the author of the Book of Acts. He provides us with two accounts of Paul's miraculous conversion, and they are different. According to the account in Acts 9, Paul's traveling companions heard a voice and saw nothing, but in Acts 22 we are told that they saw a light but heard no voice. The inconsistency is mundane, of the sort we would expect from human authors working without computers and professional editors. But it is an inconsistency, nonetheless.

---

11. The classic essay is E. D. Hirsch, Jr., *Validity in Interpretation* (New Haven: Yale, 1967). Many conservative Evangelical Christians have followed in his theoretical footsteps.

More pressing are those cases where we find theological inconsistency in an author. For example, in Galatians 3 Paul presents salvation "by faith" as an ancient element of Judaism (Abraham was saved by faith) and then tells us, in almost the same breath, that it is something new: "Now before faith came, we were confined under the law, kept under restraint until faith should be revealed" (3:23-24).[12] So, is "salvation by faith" *new,* or is it *ancient?* In another case Paul argues that God's promises to Abraham apply only to those with faith and not to Abraham's natural children (Rom 9:6-13), but a few chapters later he describes the promise as "irrevocable"; therefore, "All Israel will be saved" (11:25-32). Paul's ambiguity on these and other matters has spawned many theological and scholarly debates. Similar ambiguity appears in the Pentateuch. Although the text begins with a strong affirmation of human equality in Genesis (all human beings were taken from the same soil and bear the same divine image), the Pentateuch as a whole is replete with racial and religious prejudice. We see the results in Ezra and Nehemiah, where post-exilic Jews systematically excluded foreigners from the religious assembly and divorced their foreign wives (Ezra 9–10; Neh 13:1-3). Apparently neither the editors of the Pentateuch nor Ezra and Nehemiah realized the full implication of Genesis 1 for their treatment of foreign people.

As this last example illustrates, one reason for the Bible's inconsistency is that texts often have implicit or latent ramifications that their authors do not fully grasp, largely because human authors never have perfectly coherent understandings of everything they write about. As I will explore in greater detail later on, this observation has important implications for our theological readings of Scripture. We cannot move directly from the biblical author's discourse to Christian theology. We must evaluate the author's unique theological contribution in light of what other bib-

---

12. Augustine admitted that Paul's "apparent" inconsistency stood behind his original doubts about the Christian faith. Three modern scholars who have questioned Paul's consistency include John Drane, Hans Hübner, and Heikki Räisänen. Although Räisänen in particular takes this too far, the basic thrust of their observation — that Paul was not rigorously consistent — strikes me as right. For discussion of their views and bibliography, see Stephen Westerholm, *Perspectives Old and New on Paul: The "Lutheran" Paul and His Critics* (Grand Rapids: Eerdmans, 2004), 164-77. For Augustine's comments see *Confessions* 7.21 (NPNF1 1.114).

lical authors have said and in conversation with other God-given sources of insight.

Finally, we should note one more turn in the road of interpretation. Sensitivity to the human author's discourse is more complicated than simply attending to what one author wrote. In the case of Genesis, for instance, reading it as a piece of ancient human discourse might require that we consider the intentions of numerous authors and editors who wrote the book, as well as the perspectives of those who assembled the Pentateuch, the Hebrew canon, and the Christian Bible. We cannot simply ask, "What did the original author of Genesis mean to say with the story of Adam and Eve?" We should also ask (for example) what early Jews and Christians meant or thought when they accepted this story as a suitable introduction for their respective canonical collections. Each perspective that we can discern from the canon is useful in our quest to hear God's voice because each bears a unique perspective on what is right and true.[13]

Beyond Authorial Intention

As I have indicated already, reading the Bible as a culturally and historically situated document does not mean that we should attend only to aims of ancient authors. Good readers engage the text in a variety of ways which take us sometimes closer to, sometimes further from, the particular concerns of the biblical author.

Among the things that stand fairly close to the author, we can mention that good readings of Scripture require aesthetic competence and sensitivity. Authors often display artistic flair in their texts, and, when they do, it behooves readers to notice and appreciate it. By this an author's rhetoric hits us full force, so that we receive his or her message with utmost seriousness. But here we must be cautious. For the alluring poetry of Job and the persuasive rhetoric of Paul, however moving we find them, do not guarantee that everything they wrote was spot-on. Our aesthetically

---

13. See Brevard S. Childs, *Introduction to the Old Testament as Scripture* (Philadelphia: Fortress, 1979), 47-137.

sensitive readings of Scripture must be informed by critical theological reflection as well.

Empathy is another element in good reading. The point is not to recover an author's "intention" but rather to enter into the human situation of the author and audience. Consider, as an example, this text from Lamentations, followed by a modern Christian comment on it:

> With their own hands, compassionate women have boiled their own children, who became their food when my people were destroyed. (Lam 4:10)

> That it was the nature of these women to be compassionate simply brings home the horror of it all, for it is when evil appears in such close proximity to good that it is most shocking.[14]

What I wish to point out is the fairly casual, intellectual engagement in the commentary. The description does not err, nor is the tone objectionable, but the reading falls short as a full-orbed engagement with the text. A richer reading will go farther and deeper into the human condition, as it empathizes with the plight and tragedy of the ancient situation and, through that, with the plight of those who suffer in our own day. Unless we are so moved as readers, it is doubtful that we will respond to the biblical text in a fully human way. Reading entails the full range of human emotions and responses, so that we "rejoice with those who rejoice, and weep with those who weep" (Rom 12:15). Anything less will perhaps be useful, but it may ultimately prove superficial.

Readers can and will bring other legitimate questions to the text, in some cases questions remote from the original author's aims. What does the text tell us about the social world of ancient Jews and Christians or about the history of Israel and the church? How does the theology in this text compare with the theology in another text? What can we learn about the Hebrew, Aramaic, and Greek languages from the text? What do we learn about sociology, anthropology, and psychology from this text? And to reverse this last question, how can modern sociology, anthropology,

14. I provide no reference to underscore the fact that I intend no criticism of the author.

psychology, and theology help us understand the text, respecting both its author and audience? Though these kinds of historical, linguistic, sociological, and theological questions may be quite foreign to the intentions of the particular biblical author, the queries themselves are not objectionable and in many cases may lead to beneficial insights for readers of sacred Scripture.

Is Scripture Perspicuous?

I trust that this is enough to give readers a general impression of what I take to be an appropriate, historically sensitive approach to Scripture. I can imagine already what one concern will be. Some readers will be uncomfortable with my historical emphasis because, by bestowing priority and privilege to historically-informed, scholarly readings of Scripture, I seem to imply that non-specialists sitting in the church pew — untrained in ancient languages, culture, and history — cannot really read the Bible. So I have sacrificed the lay reader's "ordinary meaning" on the altar of scholastic priesthood.

Let us note first that, in the best sense, biblical scholarship is nothing other than an attempt to understand and make explicit the "ordinary meaning" of the biblical text.[15] When scholarship strikes us as an excessively esoteric pursuit of exotic meaning, this is mainly because historical and cultural distance has made the text's ordinary (or literal, or natural) meaning more difficult to grasp than is the case for a modern newspaper or novel. Just as uninformed readers will mistake *Gulliver's Travels* for a mere children's tale (rather than the political and intellectual work that it also is), so uninformed readers will tend to misunderstand the Bible. Even ancient readers found the Bible difficult going. The author of 2 Pet 3:16 pointed out that Paul's letters "contain some things that are hard to understand." The same is implied of Isaiah's words when the Ethiopian eunuch declared that he could not understand the prophet "unless someone guides me" (Acts 8:31). If this is true of Isaiah's prophecies and Paul's let-

---

15. As noted by Daniel M. Patte, *Ethics of Biblical Interpretation: A Reevaluation* (Louisville: Westminster John Knox, 1995), 93-94.

ters, how much more of the profundity of Jesus' parables or of the culturally remote rituals in Leviticus. The idea that Scripture's meaning is everywhere perspicuous (clear and obvious) to the average reader does not seem to be a biblical idea. And even if the Bible were perspicuous in principle, this would hardly have helped its original audiences, who in many cases were illiterate and, at any rate, did not have personal copies of the Bible on hand.[16]

I certainly do *not* intend to say that readers of the Bible must attend very carefully to the ancient context of the Bible's authors and audiences. I have only said that, among other things, we understand the biblical authors better — sometimes *much* better — when we attend to this. So everyone can read the Bible thanks to printing presses and modern educational systems (and for this "democratization" of Scripture we can be thankful), but insofar as we wish to understand the Bible's ancient discourse, it remains true that not everyone can read it equally well. The bottom line is that lay readers in our own day would not have Bibles in hand were it not for the help of those who know the ancient languages and contexts of Scripture. We *always* read Scripture with the help of specialists. This is because, in the end, the Bible simply *is* an ancient document written in Hebrew, Aramaic, and Greek. So we read it better when we take its antiquity into account.

The fact that the Bible is also a living document,[17] through which God speaks afresh in every generation of church life, is a matter that I will discuss in the chapters that follow.

16. There is an ongoing debate about literacy in ancient Israel. But even with the most optimistic estimates, books were scarce in ancient Israel and literacy was very limited by modern standards. See David W. Jamieson-Drake, *Scribes and Schools in Monarchic Judah: A Socio-Archaeological Approach* (Sheffield: JSOT Press, 1991); William M. Schniedewind, *How the Bible Became a Book: The Textualization of Ancient Israel* (Cambridge: Cambridge University Press, 2004).

17. Heb 4:12.

CHAPTER 10

Listening to the Diversity and Unity of Scripture

When we read the Bible with historical and contextual sensitivity, we notice with ease that Scripture does not speak consistently on all matters. It is a diverse book written by numerous authors and editors who addressed different audiences and social situations. Sometimes their discourses are contradictory and, in extreme cases, convey ideas that verge on what we would call vice. But Scripture also offers undeniable beauty as it encourages us to love God and neighbor with a spirit of abandon and self-sacrifice. If this is right — if Scripture speaks the truth through perceptive yet warped human horizons — then how can we use it to weave a useful and coherent understanding of God and of his relationship with us? How can the Bible, as a diverse and broken book, serve as a primary source of our theological insight? My pursuit of an answer to this important question begins below and continues into the next two chapters.

First, if we wish to take Scripture's human authors seriously, then theological interpretation necessarily includes a "two-step" process that appreciates the distinction between Scripture's human and divine discourse. Cardinal Ratzinger (now Pope Benedict) put it this way:

> [T]exts must first be restored to their historical locus and interpreted in their historical context. But this must be followed by a second phase of interpretation, however, in which they must also be seen in light of

the entire historical movement and in terms of the central event of Christ.[1]

From the Protestant side Nicholas Wolterstorff provides a similar description of theological interpretation:

> We do our interpreting for divine discourse with convictions in two hands: in one hand, our convictions as to the stance and content of the appropriated discourse and the meanings of the sentences used; in the other, our convictions concerning the probabilities and improbabilities of what God would have been intending to say by appropriating this particular discourse-by-inscription.[2]

We first listen to the human discourse and then ask what God is now saying through it. Ratzinger and Wolterstorff are well aware that we cannot do this without having already some preconceived ideas about what we can expect from divine discourse. So the two "steps" are not neatly sequential. But heuristically speaking, if we wish to exploit every theological angle that God has offered through his many biblical authors, we are wise to preserve a conceptual and practical distinction between their human voices and the divine discourse that gathers up these voices to depict a larger theological whole. By advocating this two-step process, I do not mean to advance a "special hermeneutic" for Scripture. Rather, I am saying that this is what we do when we read any text: we try to understand it and then to assess the import of its message in light of other things that we know and believe.

The two-step process highlights a basic difference between *historical criticism* as practiced by non-confessional and as practiced by confessional scholars. Non-confessional scholars do not engage the text with *faith*. They do not assume that God speaks through Scripture's individual au-

---

1. See Cardinal Joseph Ratzinger, "Biblical Interpretation in Conflict: On the Foundations and the Itinerary of Exegesis Today," in *Opening Up the Scriptures: Joseph Ratzinger and the Foundations of Biblical Interpretation*, ed. J. Granados, et al. (Grand Rapids: Eerdmans, 2008), 1-29, here p. 25.

2. Wolterstorff, *Divine Discourse: Philosophical Reflections on the Claim That God Speaks* (Cambridge: Cambridge University Press, 1995), 204.

thors, still less through the collected voices of the canon. Hence their readings of Scripture essentially involve two truncated steps, as they (step 1) try to read and understand each biblical text and then (step 2) assess its import for the academic questions that interest them. In spite of this limitation, Christian scholars often benefit from non-confessional readings because these often clarify the sense of the original human discourse.

Second, in a related matter, if we are to take *all* of Scripture seriously and to keep ourselves open to what every "jot and tittle" might be saying to us, then we should by all means avoid a pursuit of theological coherence that "covers up" the real or apparent differences in Scripture. We should not try to argue that biblical laws which allowed Israel to buy foreign slaves (Lev 25:44) fit very nicely with biblical texts that call for justice, equality, freedom, and love of neighbor. At a crucial point the two views are simply incommensurable. A better approach to Scripture was exemplified by Jesus himself, who freely admitted that his ethical teachings contrasted sharply with some of the ethical teachings in the Mosaic law: "You have heard that it was said, 'Eye for eye, and tooth for tooth.' *But I tell you*, Do not resist an evil person. If someone strikes you on the right cheek, turn to him the other also" (Matt 5:38-39). If we habitually conceal or neglect these kinds of differences, we will likely overlook important theological resources provided in the Bible. Moreover, there is a real danger that we will mistake Scripture's human vices as final words of divine wisdom. "Kill the Canaanites" will too easily become "Kill (or hate) anyone whose religious ideology threatens you." One only needs to recall Martin Luther's hatred of the Jews and his plan to rid Germany of them and the influence of his thought on German National Socialism to see how real the theological threat is.[3] Where we judge that Scripture presents God as saying or doing something he would not say or do, we should confess that "these texts tell us more about the purposes of their human authors than about the purposes of God."[4] We will simply admit that the author of Deuteronomy *wrongly believed* (as Luther did) that God told his people to slaughter their enemies. To express in theological jargon, Scrip-

3. Martin Luther, "On the Jews and Their Lies."
4. John J. Collins, "The Zeal of Phinehas: The Bible and the Legitimation of Violence," *JBL* 122 (2003): 3-21, here p. 10.

ture includes both "God-talk" (first-order words from God to humanity) and "god-talk-talk" (mistaken, second-order human accounts of what God has supposedly said. This is an important distinction that we will explore in more detail below.[5]

Third, I would maintain that the brokenness and diversity of Scripture do not negate its essential unity.[6] In saying so, I do not intend to deny the truth in Pope Benedict's judgment that, apart from our faith in the God of Scripture, "nothing is left beyond contradictory speech fragments which cannot subsequently be brought into any relation."[7] There is a sense in which, on a human level, Scripture is incoherent. Nevertheless, I would say that even apart from faith, one can sense in Scripture a narrative portrait of the human situation and of God's redemptive plan to put it right. I would attribute this coherence to the ancient authors and editors of the Bible, who were modestly "systematic" in their effort to present a coherent theological picture. This systematic tendency appears in the arrangement of the biblical canon as a whole and in some of its individual books, such as the effort of the author of Hebrews to relate the Old and New Testaments theologically.

Because of this editorial effort, Scripture from Genesis to Revelation presents a tolerably coherent story, what one scholar has called a "theodrama."[8] It begins with God's creation of the cosmos and humanity, describes the Fall of humanity and its damaging effects, testifies to God's redemptive work to put his fallen world aright through Christ, and ends

5. For this distinction between God-talk and god-talk-talk, see Alan J. Torrance, "Can the Truth Be Learned? Redressing the 'Theologistic Fallacy' in Modern Biblical Scholarship," in *Scripture's Doctrine and Theology's Bible: How the New Testament Shapes Christian Dogmatics*, ed. M. Bockmuehl and A. J. Torrance (Grand Rapids: Baker, 2008), 143-63.

6. As was accentuated in the "Scripture Project," which produced the excellent volume, Ellen F. Davis and Richard B. Hayes, eds., *The Art of Reading Scripture* (Grand Rapids: Eerdmans, 2003): see especially p. 1; Richard B. Hays, "Can Narrative Criticism Recover the Theological Unity of Scripture?" *JTI* 2 (2008): 193-211.

7. Cardinal Joseph Ratzinger, *The Nature and Mission of Theology: Approaches to Understanding Its Role in the Light of Present Controversy*, tr. A. Walker (San Francisco: Ignatius, 1995), 93-95.

8. Kevin J. Vanhoozer, *The Drama of Doctrine: A Canonical-Linguistic Approach to Christian Theology* (Louisville: Westminster John Knox, 2005); see also J. Todd Billings, *The Word of God for the People of God: An Entryway to the Theological Interpretation of Scripture* (Grand Rapids: Eerdmans, 2010), 195-228.

with predictions of Christ's return and a final reckoning of all things. Such is the general effect of Scripture's narrative shape. I do not believe that this biblical narrative should be construed mainly as a "story world" alternative to the world we live in, as some narrative theologians have suggested.[9] Rather, the Bible seeks to explain what is actually going on in *this* world, whether we realize it or not, and invites us to see *this* world in a certain way.[10] The fact the some biblical narratives depict the world as it should be in contrast to how it actually is only supports this conclusion. To be sure, as Richard Bauckham has pointed out, the biblical story's unity is "broken" and is neither complete nor perfect.[11] But again, on the whole, the coherence and shape of the biblical story give us important clues about how to organize our theology.

The shape and substance of the biblical story explicitly point us to a fourth principle for organizing our theology. Namely, our theology should grant priority to Jesus Christ, to knowing him, his teachings, and the redemptive significance of his resurrection, ascension, and eventual return.[12] As Pope Benedict expressed it, "Christ is the key to all things. . . . [O]nly by walking with Christ, by reinterpreting all things in his light, with him, crucified and risen, do we enter into the riches and beauty of sacred Scripture."[13] Benedict's point is thoroughly biblical. For the entire

9. A conceptual suggestion of "narrative theology," as espoused by Hans W. Frei, *The Eclipse of Biblical Narrative: A Study in Eighteenth and Nineteenth Century Hermeneutics* (New Haven: Yale University Press, 1974).

10. Lesslie Newbigin, "The Bible as Universal History," in *The Gospel in a Pluralist Society* (Grand Rapids: Eerdmans, 1989), 89-102.

11. Richard Bauckham, *Bible and Mission: Christian Witness in a Postmodern World* (Grand Rapids: Baker Academic, 2003), 90-94.

12. For the broad-based agreement on this point, see Ratzinger, "Biblical Interpretation in Conflict," 25; Karl Barth, *Church Dogmatics* (Edinburgh: T. & T. Clark, 1936-77), 1/2.1-202; Peter Enns, *Inspiration and Incarnation: Evangelicals and the Problem of the Old Testament* (Grand Rapids: Baker Academic, 2005), 154-59; Ray S. Anderson, "The Resurrection of Jesus as Hermeneutical Criterion," *TSF Bulletin*, January-February, 1986: 9-15, March-April, 1986: 15-22; Richard B. Hays, "Reading Scripture in Light of the Resurrection," in *The Art of Reading Scripture* (n. 5 above), 216-38.

13. From Benedict's Lenten meeting with the clergy of Rome, February 22, 2007. Quoted from Scott W. Hahn, *Covenant and Communion: The Biblical Theology of Pope Benedict XVI* (Grand Rapids: Brazos, 2009), 82.

canon of Scripture, with the first testament leading to Jesus and the second reflecting back on his life, is oriented around the revelation of God in Christ. John's Gospel, in particular, warns us not to seek life in Scripture itself but rather by embracing it as a testimony that points us to Jesus (5:39-40).

Augustine pointed out that a "christocentric" reading of Scripture will naturally emphasize Jesus' programmatic claim that love for God and neighbor sums up the whole law. But the christocentric principle has a broader application.[14] To illustrate, let us consider this little story from the book of Numbers:

> When the Israelites were in the wilderness, they found a man gathering sticks on the Sabbath day. Those who found him gathering sticks brought him to Moses, Aaron, and to the whole congregation. They put him in custody, because it was not clear what should be done to him. Then Yahweh said to Moses, "The man shall be put to death; all the congregation shall stone him outside the camp." (Num 15:32-34)

If we are at all familiar with the Gospels, we cannot help but compare this text with Mark's depiction of Jesus, who defended his disciples when they were picking and eating grains of wheat on the Sabbath. Appealing to a text in 1 Samuel, Jesus justified their actions because "The Sabbath was made for man, not man for the Sabbath" (Mark 2:27). It seems to me that the spirit of grace and freedom exemplified in the ministry of Jesus is very different from the legalism of Numbers. And a christocentric reading of Scripture will naturally prefer the approach of Jesus. For it seems that human fallibility has influenced the legal ruling of Numbers more dramatically than it has influenced the teaching of Jesus and Mark's account of it. Or, as Chrysostom expressed it, "The law, if it arrests a murderer, puts him to death. The gospel, if it arrests a murderer, enlightens and gives him life. . . . [T]his is the meaning of 'the letter kills.'"[15]

If we are to be seriously Christological, I should perhaps say some-

14. Augustine, *On Christian Doctrine* 1.39 (NPNF1 2.532-33).
15. Citing Num 15:32-34 in his discussion of 2 Corinthians 36. See Chrysostom, *Homilies on Second Corinthians* 6.2 (NPNF1 12.307).

thing about scholarly discussions of the "historical Jesus."[16] As readers may know, most biblical scholars assume that there is a difference between the historical Jesus — the Jesus who actually lived — and the portrait of his life in the Gospels. This assumption must be right to some extent, if for no other reason than the factual differences among the four biblical Gospels themselves. As a consequence of this observation, New Testament scholars have expended considerable energy trying to ascertain what we can know about the life and ministry of Jesus. Now if one thinks about this very much, a question quickly comes to mind: Is it the life and theology of Jesus himself or the biblical portrait of Jesus offered by the four Evangelists that stands as the authoritative basis for Christological interpretation?[17] It is my opinion that, ultimately, we must say that each Jesus — the historical and biblical — is authoritative in its own way. Regarding this point, a few examples are worth a thousand words.

Let us consider an important difference between John and the Synoptic Gospels. Whereas in the Synoptics Jesus preaches about the coming "kingdom of God" ("Repent, for the kingdom of God is at hand"), in John's Gospel Jesus generally preaches about *himself* ("I am the way, the truth, and the life. No one comes to the Father except by me"). If we ask which source has it right in terms of the biographical facts, biblical scholars tell us that the Synoptics are closer to the historical truth; Jesus mainly preached about the kingdom and not about himself.[18] Thus we can deduce, on the basis of this historical portrait, that Jesus was a man of spiritual humility, who understood what it means to live as a human being under the authority of God the Father. If we wish to be Christological about it, then our lives, our teaching, and our preaching will wisely emulate the humility of Jesus. That is, we shall try to live like the Jesus of history.

But what of John's Gospel? Taken as a portrait of what Jesus actually

16. For a brief introduction to and description of the contemporary scholarship on this question, see Ben Witherington III, *The Jesus Quest: The Third Search for the Jew of Nazareth* (Downers Grove, IL: InterVarsity, 1997).

17. For an insightful exploration of this theme, see Dale C. Allison, *The Historical Christ and the Theological Jesus* (Grand Rapids: Eerdmans, 2009).

18. For an introductory discussion, see Robert Kysar, "John, the Gospel of," *Anchor Bible Dictionary*, ed. D. N. Freedman (6 vols.; New York: Doubleday, 1992), 3.931.

said and did his Gospel sometimes fails us, but John portrays more clearly than the other Gospels who Jesus actually was and is: the only savior of the world, God's one and final solution through which all people are saved. Of course one might deduce this as well from the Synoptics, but the uniqueness of Jesus is more fixed in our tradition because of John's straightforward claims about Jesus. More than the other Gospel writers, John depicted the savior as the person he ultimately was rather than as the person he appeared to be in the scheme of normal history. Thus, while we should take seriously the humble Jesus of history, we should also worship Jesus as the exalted savior of the cosmos.

It is possible that our historical and theological work, based on the whole canon and other historical and theological sources, might give us a clearer understanding of Jesus Christ than any of the individual Gospel writers had. I suspect (for example) that Jesus was more traditionally Jewish than the Gospels might suggest.[19] Whether readers agree with this is not the point. I only wish to say that our judgments about the historical Jesus should bear on our theological reflection. For everything that we learn of Jesus Christ, in terms of what he said and did, and also in terms of what people have come to understand about him, should count in our Christ-centered theological deliberations.

A fifth factor in theological interpretation follows from this last observation. Where Christological interpretations of Scripture reveal the brokenness of Scripture (for example, in the contrast between Christ's love and Deuteronomy's ban), these remind us that the biblical authors were themselves finite and fallible human beings. This means that we must distinguish those points where God uses their discourse to direct us *explicitly* in appropriate and redemptive directions ("love your neighbor as yourself"; "do not kill") from those points where the text, more warped by human sinfulness, *implicitly* witnesses to a broken human situation ("kill the Canaanites"; "buy foreign slaves"). So while it is quite true that everything in Scripture coherently speaks for God *when rightly appraised*, it is equally important to keep in mind that Scripture does not everywhere speak in the same way.

19. Notice, for instance, how difficult it was for the followers of Jesus, such as Peter and James, to accept Gentiles into the Church (see Gal 2:11-12).

There is an unavoidable circularity in parsing out where God speaks explicitly in Scripture and where he speaks implicitly. How do we know that "love your neighbor" is sound and healthy and "kill the Canaanites" is warped and broken? Does our theological resistance to the extermination of Canaanites in Joshua arise from spiritual arrogance and sinful flesh — from an unwillingness to let God be God and to accept his wisdom in ordering their destruction? Or does it stem from other texts in the Old and New Testaments that teach us to take a strong stand *with God* against things like violence and genocide? If we wish to avoid sitting in God's judgment seat, this is a question that we must ask again and again as we endeavor to understand the voice of Scripture. There is no guarantee that we will answer the question correctly. We will sometimes be quite sure that we have heard from God and be wrong. But the possibility of theological and spiritual failure should not dissuade us from the pursuit of good theology and a healthy faith. Living as a Christian has never been a simple matter. It is, as Paul pointed out, a struggle that pits flesh against spirit (Galatians 5–6).

Here I should add a word of caution about our theological response to the Bible's most broken texts. When we notice that a biblical author seems to have hated his enemies, we should *never* respond in self-righteousness, as if we are somehow better people. For these dark texts are implicit and sobering reminders that we, no less than the biblical author, bear in ourselves the dangerous capacity for hatred and violence against others: all of us have our own "Canaanites." Paul reminds us that "God has consigned all men to disobedience, that he may have mercy upon all" (Rom 11:32). To stand in judgment over the authors of Deuteronomy and Joshua as if we are better people is to cast the first stone.

Sixth, as a corollary of the previous point, I wish to avoid a possible misunderstanding of the distinction between the Bible's explicit and implicit theological testimony. I am not saying that interpretation is as simple as putting some texts in the "explicit and healthy" column and others in the "implicit and broken" column. Rather, a proper organization of Scripture's teaching and testimony should appreciate that *all* biblical texts, even those most "broken" by human influence, witness truly and explicitly to what is theologically true. Let us again take up the genocide texts in Deuteronomy as an example.

We are right, I think, to notice that the biblical author's casual attitude toward genocide caused him to put words in God's mouth that were warped by human limitations. In this respect the text implicitly witnesses to what the Bible elsewhere says explicitly: that all human beings, including this biblical author, are fallen and in need of redemption. But even this text, terribly broken as it obviously is, projects for us an explicit understanding of theology. The author knows that God is holy and just, that humanity stands in rebellion against him and by right faces justice, that an all-out effort is needed to eradicate evil from a fallen world, that God himself will ultimately secure this victory, and that those who trust God can yearn for his victory. All this is offered by this key episode in the biblical drama.[20] Also, if biblical scholars are right, then the author of Deuteronomy was not as sour on his enemies as it first seems. The author wrote in the days of King Josiah, when no living Canaanites existed.[21] So his anti-Canaanite rhetoric was really directed against Canaanite *religion* and not against human beings themselves. When confronting actual flesh-and-blood enemies, the author instructed Israel to offer terms of peace (Deut 20:10). So the author of Deuteronomy — who elsewhere defended the cause of widows, orphans, and aliens — was a far softer fellow than the genocide texts suggest. If we are to hear him speak, we must hear *everything* he has to say, both the good and the ugly.

Seventh, given that every biblical text is a partial window into God's truth (although some windows are open more widely than others), one way to conceptualize Scripture is as a collection of texts that, *when embraced as a canonical whole,* tends to direct and push us in appropriate directions.[22]

---

20. For a recent effort to distill the theological fruit in Deuteronomy, see Douglas S. Earl, "The Christian Significance of Deuteronomy 7," *JTI* 3 (2009): 41-62.

21. This will be true even if Deuteronomy was written decades earlier in the days of Hezekiah (as some scholars believe). For a basic introduction to the date of Deuteronomy, see Moshe Weinfeld, *Deuteronomy 1–11* (AB; New York: Doubleday, 1991), 1-122.

22. Emphasis on "canonical" readings of Scripture goes back in different ways to scholars like Karl Barth, Hans Frei, and (especially) Brevard Childs, who in their respective ways encouraged Christians to read the Bible as a whole. Their insights have been embraced and further developed by just about every scholar working in the area of "theological interpretation." For a brief introduction to Childs's work on canonical reading, see Christopher Seitz, "Canonical Approach," in *Dictionary for Theological Interpretation of Scripture*, ed. C. G. Bartholomew, et al. (Grand Rapids: Baker, 2005), 100-102.

But this canonical effect is really cumulative, so that any one text, if taken alone as the final voice of Scripture, might seriously lead us astray. Some texts accentuate (or over-accentuate) the justice and judgment of God, while others highlight his love, grace, and patience. It is as if, for every text that seems to push us too far in one direction, another comes along that turns us back.[23] Humanity is evil and depraved, but it is good and bears God's image; children are born in sin, but they are born innocent; pagan idolaters are without excuse, but God patiently overlooks their sins; human beings have the capacity to keep God's law, or they certainly cannot keep the law; God's people must be circumcised, or they need not and even should not be circumcised; foreigners are excluded from God's people or absolutely must be included; women are property of their husbands, or they are equal. This is a list that could be expanded very easily. Healthy theology requires that we are familiar with all of Scripture and that we rightly discern how its various and untidy elements contribute to a useful theological whole.

I would add that "rightly discerning" how canonical texts relate to each other is not simply a matter of "getting at the truth." It also involves "weighing out" the relative importance of the practical and theological issues involved. Which issues are more central to Scripture and which are peripheral matters of Christian conscience? As an example, consider the view of some conservative Christians that women should be excluded from ordination to the ministry. Even if they were right, would it be so tragic if other Christians nevertheless ordained women? Would the result be more serious than, say, a male pastor who is poorly gifted for the ministry, or worse than a church soaked in materialism? My point is not that two theological wrongs make a right. My point is that all Christian traditions admit that some theological matters are more important than others.[24] And it is always possible that our theological *affirmations*, even where correct, have not been properly ordered in terms of healthy theological *priorities*. Good theology should order *and prioritize* its theological judgments.

23. As James A. Sanders pointed out, "the canon always contains the seed of redemption of any abuse of it." See his *Canon and Community: A Guide to Canonical Criticism* (Philadelphia: Fortress, 1984), 37.

24. As John Barton has noted in *People of the Book? The Authority of the Bible in Christianity* (Louisville: Westminster/John Knox, 1988), 26.

The task of rightly relating the Bible's diverse texts to each other is fostered by an eighth element in our theological reading of Scripture, which usually goes by names like "progressive revelation," "redemptive history" or, more recently, "trajectory theology." The approach reflects a belief that, in the nature of things, God's continuing conversation with humanity gradually unfolds within the emerging contours of history. God speaks first through creation, then through the Old Testament, then in Christ, then in the New Testament, and then through the ever-present and continuing voice of his Spirit (including its activity in and through the Church). It is fairly easy to see that there must be *something* right in this progressive understanding of divine discourse, both logically and substantively.[25] Logically, whenever God speaks to us, it goes with the territory that there is some measure of "progress" in our understanding of God. Substantively, the different portraits of God and religion provided in the Old and New Testaments also suggest progress. As the author of Hebrews expressed it, the Old Testament law is "only a shadow of the good things to come and not the true form of these realities" (Heb 10:1). John's Gospel similarly declared that "the law was given through Moses, but grace and truth came through Jesus Christ" (John 1:17).

If this is right, then good theology should try to discern the direction or trajectory of God's voice and take its stand at the end of that trajectory. On the question of circumcision, for example, the early church did not side with texts that seemed to demand circumcision (e.g., Gen 17:10; Exod 12:48) but rather with those that declared us free from the requirement (e.g., Gen 15:6; Deut 28:12; Isa 54:1; cf. Acts 15; Romans 10; Gal 5:2). Many similar examples could be cited. In these cases the things formerly indicated by Scripture reflect either the limitations or disordering influences of the human condition, else there would be no occasion for other (usually later) biblical texts to offer different judgments.

Regarding our use of trajectory theology, I would offer two words of caution. First, though the Old and New Testaments give us somewhat dif-

---

25. Here I part ways with Edgar V. McKnight, who argues that "progressive revelation" depends conceptually on Enlightenment notions of "progress." See Edgar V. McKnight, *Postmodern Use of the Bible: The Emergence of Reader-Oriented Criticism* (Nashville: Abingdon, 1988), 67-69.

ferent overall impressions of God, it remains the case that the Old Testament anticipated the best of Christian ethics (see my comments in chapter 6). So by all means, trajectory theology is not a naïve expression of "supersessionism," the idea that the Old Testament is essentially inferior and largely irrelevant to Christian theology. This theological idea has been very popular in the annals of church history, in both the early and modern periods, but those who embrace it have failed to appreciate the important connections between Old and New Testament theology and ethics. Second, in a related matter, I would point out that trajectory theology, whatever it may mean, cannot mean that divine discourse always follows a chronologically progressive line. God's most complete act of self-revelation appeared *between* the testaments, in the person of Christ, rather than at Scripture's end. And because the Bible's human authors were finite and fallen men, each with his own weaknesses and blind spots, we cannot gainsay the possibility that on some matters the redemptive insight is greater in earlier texts. As an example, I would say that the theological portrait of marriage in Genesis 2 is somewhat healthier than Paul's advice (based on his limited perspective) that we forego marriage in anticipation of Christ's imminent return (1 Corinthians 7).

There will be a concern, especially among more conservative Christians, that trajectory theology will easily lead us "wherever the winds of secular culture blow." This is an understandable and very reasonable concern, and we should make every effort to insure that our theological work does not simply imitate the latest social fashions. The Bible often challenges Jews and Christians to conduct themselves with distinction. At the same time, we really must admit that trajectory theology has always been far-reaching and surprising to those on the conservative side of theology. Trajectory theology led the early (largely Jewish) church to embrace uncircumcised Gentiles, and it led later Christians to renounce slavery and polygamy, two social institutions that were permitted in both Testaments. And in the case of slavery, it was indeed the "winds of culture," especially the Enlightenment critics of Christianity, that contributed to our understanding of human freedom.[26] So we cannot easily

26. See Claudine Hunting, "The Philosophes and Black Slavery," *Journal of the History of Ideas* 39 (1978): 405-18. I would point out that Enlightenment philosophy was in many ways

say beforehand where (or how) the Spirit might lead us as it guides us in reading Scripture.

Though I have not spelled it out up to this point, the foregoing discussion of trajectory theology implies another (ninth) principle that should be at work in our reading of Scripture, namely, that a healthy use of Scripture should recognize that good theology cannot depend on Scripture only. Two examples will suffice to ground this point, one scientific and the other ethical.

On the scientific front, we should recall that in connection with the Copernican Revolution, the church rejected the cosmological insights of Copernicus and Galileo because their views did not suit Scripture. As Melanchthon expressed it, Copernicus was "a fool who wishes to reverse the entire science of astronomy; but sacred Scripture tells us that Joshua commanded the sun to stand still, and not the earth."[27] Melanchthon found support for his views in Eccl 1:5, which tell us that "the sun rises and the sun goes down, and hastens to the place where it rises." His comments are merely representative of general trends in the sixteenth century, as clergymen feverishly searched the Bible line by line for passages that would confirm the traditional, earth-centered view of the cosmos.[28] Viewed from our modern vantage point, the sixteenth-century predicament is obvious: if one *must* embrace a cosmology that suits the biblical view, then all the scientific evidence, however clear and coherent, must be set aside in favor of an earth-centered cosmos. Of course the church eventually managed to embrace the new view by either admitting that the Bible was not a science book or by arguing (awkwardly) that the Bible really did teach Copernican cosmology. But my main point is that, in this case, the church was only able to get at the right answer by finally allowing the scientific evidence to "trump" biblical views of the cosmos.

On the ethical front we have the problem of slavery. Though it is quite

informed by gospel teachings about love and equality. So it was not reason alone, but reason informed by Scripture, that pointed critics in the right direction.

27. Melanchthon, *Initia Doctrinae Physicae*. English quotation from A. D. White, *The History of the Warfare of Science with Theology in Christendom* (2 vols.; New York: Appleton, 1920), 1.126.

28. Thomas S. Kuhn, *The Copernican Revolution* (Cambridge: Harvard University Press, 1957), 192.

true that the lot of slaves improved in the New Testament as compared to the Old Testament, the fact remains that the Bible never arrived explicitly at the appropriate ethical step of full emancipation. An unfortunate result is that the Christian West required many centuries to end its barbaric trade in human beings. Christians who stood at the forefront of the emancipation movement did so because, in their view, the biblical injunctions to "love your neighbor as yourself" and to "do unto others," coupled with Paul's appeal that Philemon release his slave, pointed us in the proper ethical direction.[29] So, although Scripture did not advance an argument for full emancipation of slaves, we can reasonably deduce that its theological trajectory *pointed* toward that end.

Scripture was not intended to stand alone as *the* criterion by which theological and ethical judgments are made.[30] Hence, Christian theology, as it reads and seeks to follow Scripture, must be ready to move beyond Scripture in some cases.[31] And when it does so, this theological move is not foreign to the Bible but rather invited by it. That is, paradoxical as it might sound, it is quite biblical to go beyond the Bible. The goal of biblically informed theology is not merely to go where the Scripture goes: we must also be ready to go where God, through Scripture, is pointing.

29. John Wesley, *The Works of John Wesley* (12 vols.; London: Wesleyan Methodist Book Room, 1872), 11.59-79.

30. William J. Abraham, *Canon and Criterion* (Oxford: Oxford University Press, 1998).

31. As even evangelical Christians increasingly admit. See I. Howard Marshall, *Beyond the Bible: Moving from Scripture to Theology* (Grand Rapids: Baker, 2004); William J. Webb, *Slaves, Women, and Homosexuals: Exploring the Hermeneutics of Cultural Analysis* (Downers Grove, IL: InterVarsity, 2001).

CHAPTER 11

Theology beyond the Bible:
Spirit, Cosmos, Tradition, and Experience

I f Christian theology should consider other evidence besides the Bible in its deliberations, and in cases move beyond Scripture's discourse in some form or fashion, to what other "voices" must we attend? Space does not permit a full-orbed answer to this question, but I would like to offer three important *biblical* answers to the question.

The Voice of the Spirit

The church must "listen to what the Spirit is saying to the churches" (Rev 2:7, etc.). The Spirit's voice is repeatedly accentuated in the New Testament. It convinces the world "concerning sin and righteousness and judgment" (John 16:7-8). It bears witness "with our spirit" that we are children of God (Rom 8:16). The Spirit "leads us" (Rom 8:14) and "helps us in our weakness" (v. 26), and by it we have and exercise spiritual gifts for the encouragement of the church (Romans 12 and 1 Corinthians 12). In Acts the Spirit speaks directly to human beings, not only to the apostles (Acts 10:19) but also to "lay" Christians and to unbelievers (8:29; 10:1-3; 22:9-10). The Spirit is in some sense the divine author of Scripture, both in inspiring its human authors (2 Pet 1:20-21) and in speaking through the text itself (Heb 3:7). So if we take the Bible with any seriousness we will recognize that the voice of the Spirit is a crucial voice in the church's theological reflection.

Scripture suggests that the Spirit's voice is articulated in at least two modes, as it were. First, the Spirit is constantly at work in the human situation, among believers and unbelievers, speaking with a still small voice. In this mode the Spirit brings thoughts to mind, guides us to the truth, and even prays to the Father on our behalf, compensating in some way for the warped articulations and inadequacies of our own prayers (Rom 8:26-27).[1] Like the apostle Paul, we should accept this as comforting news that God is at work in the hearts of human beings.

Secondly, there is a sense in which the Spirit speaks through its visible activity. The church's earliest "ecumenical" council, in Acts 15, provides a vivid example. It was a contentious meeting, as pro-Gentile and pro-Jewish factions sorted out their theological differences about the Jewish law.[2] The Jewish party believed that all Gentile converts should convert to Jewish Christianity by receiving circumcision; for *very* obvious reasons, the Gentile party disagreed. Both sides could cite Scripture in support of their view, but it must have seemed that the Jewish party's position was much stronger. Circumcision is a central rite in the Hebrew canon, and the text explicitly describes it as an "eternal covenant" (Gen 17:13) to be observed by Jews and, most importantly, by any foreigners who wished to join Judaism (Gen 17:27; Exod 12:48). Nevertheless, in a decision that must have surprised and befuddled the Jewish party, the council finally decided that the Gentiles could become Christians without circumcision and without observing the Jewish law. This decision was partly based on Scripture, but the deciding factor, according to Acts, was that the Gentiles had received the gift of the Holy Spirit without circumcision. So the Holy Spirit's "voice" (its supernatural activity) tilted the theological scale in the direction of the pro-Gentile party. The weaker position from Scripture, supported by the Spirit, bested the stronger position opposed by the Spirit.

The bottom line is that Scripture, tradition, and experience teach and demonstrate that God animates his church through the life and activity of

1. See John Ziesler, *Paul's Letter to the Romans* (London: SCM Press, 1989), 223-24; Karl Barth, *The Epistle to the Romans* (6th ed.; Oxford: Oxford University Press, 1968), 315-17; Martin Luther, *Commentary on Romans* (Grand Rapids: Zondervan, 1954), 126.

2. The example is from Stephen E. Fowl, *Engaging Scripture: A Model for Theological Interpretation* (Malden, MA: Blackwell, 1998), 97-113.

the Spirit. This undoubtedly explains how the church manages to exist and prosper in so many cultural and social contexts.[3] Anyone who has attended a Lausanne Conference, which brings together Christians from so many lands, will testify to the way that the Spirit unifies the church while affirming its culturally distinctive expressions. The Spirit's work is mysterious, but the results are palpable.

If the Spirit's activity is a dependable theological compass, why not simply dispense with Scripture and "let the Spirit lead"? This is an approach that has been advocated in some theological circles,[4] but it has at least three obvious strikes against it. First, as Augustine long ago pointed out, those who advocate a simple "Spirit-led" approach inevitably assume that *they* ought to *teach* others their spiritual and theological insights.[5] So it would seem that God's use of human mediation in his self-communication is unavoidable and indispensable. Second, though we should and must grant that the Spirit speaks in some way or other, this affirmation does not resolve our hermeneutical problems. Anyone who has walked the Christian path for very long knows how easy it is to warp the Spirit's voice so that we hear from it what we wish. One thinks here of Job's friend Eliphaz, who mistakenly believed that a spirit from God had confirmed his errant theology (Job 4:12-21). Third, Scripture presents the Spirit's activity as closely related to God's written word and to those who teach it. God sent Philip — not the Spirit alone — to help an Ethiopian understand the book of Isaiah (Acts 8:26-40). While I have no desire to say what God can and cannot do in particular situations, it seems to me that the Spirit's activity in God's self-disclosure, and in his guidance of the church, is closely tied to Scripture.

The fact that the Spirit speaks through the creaturely text of Scripture suggests that the Spirit's voice (as a rule) does not pass to us directly. It is mediated through creaturely means, not only through Scripture but

3. J. Todd Billings, *The Word of God for the People of God: An Entryway to the Theological Interpretation of Scripture* (Grand Rapids: Eerdmans, 2010), 109-22.

4. Schwenkfeldian theology being a good example. See John Webster, *Holy Scripture: A Dogmatic Sketch* (Cambridge: Cambridge University Press, 2003), 109. See also Casper Schwenkfeld, "Verantwortung und Gegenbericht" (1554), in *Corpus Schwenkfeldianorum*, ed. D. Hartranft, et al. (Leipzig: Breitkopf and Härtel, 1907-61), 13.987.

5. Augustine, *On Christian Doctrine*, Preface (NPNF1 2.520).

also through the created order, the testimony of others, and the insights of rationality, memory, and conscience. So there are many ways for the Spirit to speak. Nevertheless, the Spirit speaks especially through Scripture, which concretely instantiates, through particular contextual viewpoints, those things that are fundamentally important for the faith. It was for this very benefit that the church assembled and embraced a written canon.

In the end, I suspect that we cannot say with much precision how the Spirit, who "comes and goes as he pleases" (John 3:8), works as he assists us in our theological reflection. On this question Scripture does not provide much grist for our systematic theological mills. But perhaps the important point is not deeply cognitive. Perhaps it is only that God has given us the gift of the Holy Spirit as a resource for a life that is fruitful and healthy. So we can be confident that, as we pray for the Spirit's guidance when we read Scripture, we shall receive it (Jas 1:5).

The Voice of the Cosmos

Scripture expresses theology in metaphors drawn from the created order. God is our "Father" and "King," Jesus Christ is the "Son," the church is the "bride," Christians are "adopted children," unbelievers are "lost sheep," and so on. So the cosmos, both cultural and natural, provides a kind of foundation for expressing biblical truth. Aquinas was most wise, then, when he pointed out that "meditation on the divine works is necessary for instruction of faith," and "mistakes about creatures lead to mistaken knowledge about God."[6]

Scripture adds its voice to the observations of Aquinas: "The heavens are telling the glory of God; and the firmament proclaims his handiwork. Day to day pours forth speech, and night to night declares knowledge. . . . Their voice goes out through all the earth, and their words to the end of the earth" (Ps 19:1-4; cf. Rom 10:18). God's creation reflects his knowledge and wisdom and, therefore, those who study and understand the cosmic

---

6. *Contra Gentiles* 2.2-3. See Thomas Aquinas, *Summa Contra Gentiles*, tr. J. F. Anderson (3 vols. in 4; Notre Dame, IN: University of Notre Dame Press, 1975), 2.30-34.

order gain divine wisdom (see Prov 8:1-33).[7] A poignant illustration of this point is found in Prov 22:17–24:22, where the editor of Proverbs took up an older Egyptian wisdom text and, recognizing it as wise and true, adopted it as an expression of Yahweh's wisdom.[8] One implication is that everything human beings learn, whether from the practical experiences of everyday life or from academic disciplines like chemistry, biology, and psychology, may provide vital resources for our theological reflection. It does not matter much whether those insights come from Christians or from unbelievers. Truth is truth, no matter who notices it.[9] So the Christian pursuit of knowledge should never be a parochial enterprise that ignores the concerns and insights of the wider community of human persons, who as "God's offspring" are children of Adam's family. If we ignore this point, the great risk is that we will forge a "ghetto theology" whose dogmas are foreign to the real world in which we live and minister.

A current example of the creation's theological relevance is provided by the on-going debate among conservative Christians about biological evolution. The debate often pits "Scripture" against "science," as if "God's word" (which supposedly advances a literal six-day creation) stands in conflict with "human wisdom" (which advances the theory that humanity developed at the end of a long, natural biological process). But if creation is in itself a word from God, then this mode of framing the debate is quite misleading. A more appropriate description would hold that "*human interpretations* of God's written word" appear to be in conflict with "*human interpretations* of God's word in the cosmos." Good theology should attend carefully to the voices of both Scripture and the cosmos, with full awareness that *both* are subject to fallible interpretation and have been distorted

7. See Prov 8:22-36. The classic discussion is still Gerhard von Rad, *Wisdom in Israel*, tr. J. D. Martin (London: SCM Press, 1972): see especially pp. 144-76.

8. The text is known as the "Instructions of Amenemope." For references to the text, translations, and bibliography, see Kenton L. Sparks, *Ancient Texts for the Study of the Hebrew Bible: A Guide to the Background Literature* (Peabody, MA: Hendrickson, 2005), 70-71; John A. Emerton, "The Teaching of Amenemope and Proverbs xxii17-xxiv22: Further Reflections on a Long-Standing Problem," *Vetus Testamentum* 51 (2001): 431-65.

9. As Augustine expressed it, "Let every good and true Christian understand that wherever truth may be found, it belongs to his Master." *On Christian Doctrine* 2.18 (NPNF1 2.545); cf. 2.40, 42.

by the effects of fallen humanity. When we embrace creation as Scripture's divinely ordained partner in revealing truth, we avoid the blunder committed in the days of Copernicus and Galileo, when those who supposedly stood on the side of "Scripture" were wrong and those who stood on the side of "Science" were right. Insofar as the church has learned this lesson, it will be in a position to exploit the veritable explosion of new twenty-first-century insights now coming our way from scientific and social-scientific research.

Our discussion of creation and theology brings us organically into a discussion of "natural theology" or "natural revelation." Does the created order convey or reveal anything of substance about theology, and if so, how much? The classic debate on this question was framed by Karl Barth and Emil Brunner. Barth held that there is no such thing as "natural theology," whereas Brunner held that some theological truths are commonly understood through human contact with nature. I cannot explore this matter in any great detail but would most assuredly side with Brunner on the question. First, as Pannenberg has pointed out, Brunner's is the traditional Christian view.[10] It was only in the twentieth century that serious questions were raised about natural theology. And secondly, the Bible often depends on or describes the theological witness of creation.[11] Old Testament wisdom teaches that human beings acquire knowledge of God's wisdom by studying creation.[12] Other texts tell us that human beings are naturally aware of God's existence and holiness and of the fact that we should worship God (Acts 17, Romans 1). This natural theology is not superficial, for Scripture further teaches that human beings know enough of theology and ethics *without the Bible* to make us culpable before God in his tribunal of eternal justice. This is the very basis of Paul's argument in Romans that the Jews, who have the written law, are essentially in the same situation as the Gentiles who have the law written in their conscience

---

10. Wolfhart Pannenberg, *Systematic Theology* (3 vols.; Grand Rapids: Eerdmans, 1991-98), 1.73-82.

11. James Barr, *Biblical Faith and Natural Theology* (Oxford: Clarendon, 1993). See also John Barton, *Amos' Oracles against the Nations* (Cambridge: Cambridge University Press, 1980); idem, "Natural Law and Poetic Justice in the Old Testament," *Journal of Theological Studies* 30 (1979): 1-14.

12. See my previous discussion.

(Rom 2:14-15). If Paul is right about this, then either God is petty (holding us eternally culpable for things we do not know) or we really do understand something significant about the fundamentals of theology and ethics.

The created order provides the essential context for Scripture's discourse and for God's revelation in Christ, so its evidence should figure prominently in our interpretation of Scripture and in our theological deliberations.

The Voice of Tradition

I have argued already in chapter 7 that human tradition is an unavoidable and indispensable element in every engagement that produces understanding. At this point I am interested not in tradition *per se* but more narrowly in the Christian tradition itself, and in the valuable role that it plays in the theological interpretation of Scripture.

Scripture encourages us to attend closely to the witness of Christian tradition: "So then, brothers and sisters, stand firm and hold fast to the *traditions* that you were taught by us, either by word of mouth or by our letter" (2 Thess 2:15; cf. 1 Cor 11:2).[13] Does this text, and others like it, suggest that we should listen only to the oral and written apostolic tradition (a narrow understanding of tradition), or does it establish a more general pattern to follow, namely, that we should attend carefully to the apostolic tradition *as the later church has faithfully refined and developed it* (a broad understanding of tradition)?

I do not believe that Paul himself, anticipating as he did the imminent appearance of Christ (see 1 Corinthians 7), thought much about the longevity of the Christian tradition. But other texts, most particularly the book of Acts, are instructive here. As many scholars have pointed out, the author of Acts (Luke, perhaps) wrote at a time when Christians were beginning to realize that the kingdom of God would not appear right away.[14] As a result, he envisioned history as a sphere of the Spirit's work

---

13. For a discussion of this text and other issues sensitive to evangelical concerns about tradition, see D. H. Williams, *Evangelicals and Tradition: The Formative Influence of the Early Church* (Grand Rapids: Baker, 2005), especially pp. 32-39.

14. One notices, for instance, how Luke edited his source in Mark to make the end of time

and hence believed that Christian history constituted an important theological resource for the church.[15] Included in his history is an account of the first church council and its very important "Spirit-guided" theological decision regarding Gentile Christianity (Acts 15). There the church decided that Gentiles could be Christians without accepting circumcision and life under Jewish law. By embracing the significance of Christian history and by accepting the authority of this early council, the author of Acts took church tradition seriously. Should we follow his example by taking later, post-biblical church decisions and traditions seriously?

Following the pattern in Acts, the Catholic and Eastern Orthodox churches have always embraced a "broad" understanding of tradition and have held (in somewhat different ways) that the church's ongoing theological traditions are essential elements in good theology. Traditional Protestants usually embrace a narrower understanding of tradition (such as "whatever the Bible says"), but this narrow perspective is now a matter of considerable debate. In recent years, many Protestant scholars have moved in a more Catholic direction by affirming the importance of church tradition for our theological reflection. Even scholars in conservative Protestant circles are asking, "Is the Reformation over?"[16] There are a number of reasons for this development.

seem less imminent. For example, Mark wrote: "there are some standing here who will not taste death before they see that the kingdom of God has come *with power*," whereas Luke's version eliminates the phrase "with power" (Mark 9:1; Luke 9:27). For discussion, see Joseph A. Fitzmyer, *The Gospel According to Luke* (2 vols., AB; New York: Doubleday, 1981-85), 1.18-22, 786.

15. See Joseph A. Fitzmyer, *The Acts of the* Apostles (AB; New York: Doubleday, 1998), 193; Jaroslav Pelikan, *Acts* (Grand Rapids: Brazos, 2005), 50-51; Joel B. Green, "Acts of the Apostles," in *Dictionary of the Later New Testament and Its Developments*, ed. R. P. Martin and P. H. Davids (Downers Grove, IL: InterVarsity, 1997), 7-24, especially 19.

16. See James J. Buckley and David S. Yeago, "A Catholic and Evangelical Theology?" in *Knowing the Triune God: The Work of the Spirit in the Practices of the Church*, ed. J. J. Buckley and D. S. Yeago (Grand Rapids: Eerdmans, 2001), 1-20; Scot McKnight, "From Wheaton to Rome: Why Evangelicals Become Roman Catholic," *JETS* 45 (2002): 451-72; Mark A. Noll and Carol Nystrom, *Is the Reformation Over? An Evangelical Assessment of Contemporary Roman Catholicism* (Grand Rapids: Baker, 2005); Christopher R. Seitz, *Nicene Christianity: The Future for a New Ecumenism* (Grand Rapids: Brazos, 2001); Geoffrey Wainwright, *Is the Reformation Over? Catholics and Protestants at the Turn of the Millennia* (Milwaukee: Marquette University Press, 2000); Williams, *Evangelicals and Tradition*.

The early church assembled the biblical canon by choosing which books would be included and which would not. This was not done by the apostles themselves but rather by early Christians over the course of some four centuries of church history. So whenever we Protestants open our Bibles to read them, we embrace implicitly the validity of the Catholic and Orthodox traditions.[17] Tradition simply cannot be avoided: it is already with us as a sphere of human activity sanctified by God, through the Holy Spirit, to serve his purposes.

A better construal of the relationship between church and Scripture would run like this: the church stands in relation to the canon as Paul stands in relation to his letters. Just as Paul was the author of Romans, so the church was the *human author* of the canon. And this observation reinforces the importance of tradition. For if we wish to know what the church intended to "say" with its canon, we shall have to attend contextually to the kinds of things the church was saying in those early days. Foremost, we know that the early church was attempting in the canon, and in other texts, to express its theological judgments about the fundamentals and essentials of Christian doctrine. Scripture itself did not summarize these judgments in any formal and convenient way, so the church found it expedient to distill these essential doctrines in numerous creedal statements that defined the boundaries between "orthodoxy" (right belief) and "heterodoxy" (wrong belief). One thinks here of the Apostles' Creed, the Nicene Creed, and the Definition of Chalcedon, but there are others. These creeds established once and for all that Jesus was both divine and human, that he rose from the dead, and that his identity should be understood in terms of the Holy Trinity. Even Protestants have taken this orthodox "Rule of Faith" very seriously. So whether we admit it or not, in actual practice everyone in the church assumes that God has spoken and does still speak through the unfolding traditions of the church.

Another factor in the resurgence of Christian tradition among Protestants is the postmodern philosophical observation that Protestantism is itself a tradition, and a relatively new tradition at that. Given that this is the case, it is very natural for postmodern Protestants to take the older tradi-

---

17. For discussion, see Craig D. Allert, *A High View of Scripture? The Authority of the Bible and the Formation of the New Testament Canon* (Grand Rapids: Baker, 2007).

tions of Catholicism and Orthodoxy more seriously. Unless we do, we are compelled to admit that God's church was hopelessly confused and disoriented until the Protestants finally showed up to "set things right." A preferable understanding of the Reformation (in my opinion) would see the Protestants as having served a constructive theological role by exposing the corruption and errors in sixteenth-century Catholic tradition and by insisting on a more biblical basis for theological reflection. Many improvements were made on the Catholic side because of this. Nonetheless, like Scripture itself, the Christian tradition always has been and remains to this day a broken tradition. God has sanctified this broken church as his bearer of truth in the economy of grace. So whether we are Protestant, Catholic or Orthodox — or perhaps nowadays a little of all three — we have something valuable to say to, and to learn from, our brothers and sisters in the other branches of the church.

I have said that tradition should be taken "seriously." But what, precisely, does this mean? Does ecclesial tradition function as an *authority* that we must accept in every case (a Catholic position), or does it function mainly in an *advisory* role, such that we should attend to it but need not accept it as a whole (a Protestant position)?

My own sense (as a small-c "catholic" with Protestant roots) is that the Christian "tradition" is not a single authoritative voice so much as a family of closely related traditions that have different but overlapping judgments about Scripture, theology, and Christian practice. Taken together these traditions serve an authoritative role, but no single tradition holds all the cards. In a paradoxical way, this might suggest that tradition is best understood as "authoritative advice." It is "advice" insofar as it is inconsistent and cannot be accepted at face value, but it remains "authoritative" insofar as we must listen to it as best we can, allowing its many and varied Spirit-guided voices to influence the contours of our faith and practice. So, as an example, although I am not Roman Catholic and do not assume that the Catholic Church's magisterial voice speaks infallibly, I do attend carefully to its catechism as I reflect on the meaning of Scripture.

Is there is a theological "bottom line" that provides a foundation for biblical interpretation in this ecumenical age? Undoubtedly we come close to this with the traditional "Rule of Faith," to which I earlier referred, but I would caution that even this creedal foundation does not provide a failsafe guide for interpreting Scripture. There are two reasons for this. First, although the creeds are not mere advice, neither are they necessarily errorless authority. As an example, although I fully subscribe to the basic assertions of the great ecumenical creeds, I take issue with the *Anathema* pronouncements in some versions of them, which openly declare that dissenters are destined for eternal punishment. As Wesley pointed out, it may be that Christ has redeemed the heretic Pelagius.[18] Similarly, I do not wholly agree with Article XX of Anglicanism's Thirty-Nine Articles, which states that the church may not "so expound one place of Scripture that it be repugnant to another." While this certainly applies to Scripture's divine discourse and to Christian teaching (since God cannot contradict himself), I do not think that this demand can be made of Scripture's human discourse, because it is diverse. My subtle distinction between Scripture's human and divine discourse is, of course, not something that would have occurred to the sixteenth-century framers of the Articles. The main point is that creeds and catechisms can be interrogated when necessary and, hence, do not exert *carte blanche* control on our biblical exegesis and theological reflection.

The creeds cannot control our biblical exegesis for another reason. To make my point, let us consider an important and influential article by David Yeago. Yeago tries to show that Paul's theology of the incarnation in Philippians dovetails very nicely with the dogmas of the Nicene Creed.[19] His judgment on this matter contrasts with the readings of many biblical scholars, who tend to see differences between the views expressed by Paul and the Creed. Yeago's arguments are often cited precisely because they part ways with standard biblical scholarship.

Yeago may be right in this particular case, but an implication of his article seems to be that this is how it *must* turn out: Paul *must* agree with Nicea. It is with this implication that I disagree. While it is theologically convenient to assume that the Bible's ancient authors always taught in conformity with the creeds of Christian orthodoxy, I would argue that there might be a significant difference between what one biblical author

---

18. *The Works of John Wesley*, 6.328-29.

19. David S. Yeago, "The New Testament and the Nicene Dogma: A Contribution to the Recovery of Theological Exegesis," *Pro Ecclesia* 3 (1994): 152-64.

has written about the incarnation and what the later church, with the whole canon in front of it and a few centuries of experience behind it, has decided to say. Paul lived several centuries before the decisions at Nicea. Although his letters certainly influenced Nicea's theological deliberations, it is anachronistic to imagine that the theological judgments of Paul *necessarily* agreed with substantive decisions made centuries after he lived. Individual biblical authors should not be expected to agree with everything that the church has said or will say in matters of theology. And this is a good thing. For it means that the biblical authors can challenge rather than always support the traditions of the church. Unless we admit this, it seems hollow to speak of the Bible's authority over the church.

I should point out that our engagement with tradition is not restricted to great matters of church history and the three branches of Christendom. Tradition meets us in local church settings, as believers live within and are nurtured by a family or congregation of other believers. It is here, in the concrete circumstances of everyday life, that our readings of Scripture and our carefully considered theologies are tested for cogency. Does our reading of Scripture, and the resulting praxis, form Christians into people who love God and neighbor? That is the important question. Mine is not a book on spiritual formation or ecclesiology as such, but readers should be aware that, when we speak of the Christian community, we touch on the tip of a large and important theological iceberg.

The Voice of Experience

I return now to a subject covered in our chapter on epistemology, namely, *experience*. Here I wish to extend what was earlier said by asking about the role of experience in our theological reflection. For the sake of clarity, I should point out that I am referring here to "experience" in the broadest sense — to religious experience, such as we sometimes associate with mysticism, as well as to the experiences of everyday life, whether empirical (perceiving the external world) or introspective (perceiving my own thoughts and ideas). When experience is understood in this way, it clearly stands in close relation to the other topics discussed here (the Spirit, cosmos, and tradition) and also in close relation to Scripture. Our contact with the Spirit, cosmos, and tradition is always in the context of personal experience in some way or other. As I proceed here, my aim is not to provide a comprehensive discussion of the topic. I hope instead to push open a door that is already ajar by explaining why experience is important and by casting some light on its role in our theological reflection.

As I mentioned in the former discussion, experience is interpreted through the lens of tradition, but it also provides the basis for our questions about tradition.[20] This is because, where tradition errs, it sooner or later happens that the life experience does not fit the expectations of tradition. Psalm 89 provides a vivid illustration of my point. At one time its author embraced the traditional belief that King David's family would rule from Judah's throne forever (Ps 89:19-37; cf. 2 Samuel 7), but this expectation was disappointed when the Babylonian exile brought the kingdom of Judah to an abrupt end. As a result, the psalmist and like-minded Judeans were essentially forced to modify their theological belief in a "permanent" Davidic kingdom.

Most Christians would confess to similar experiences, in which the circumstances of everyday life have collided with our long-held beliefs. As a personal example I would cite my own pilgrimage respecting Catholicism. The Protestant tradition in which I was raised denied that Catholics could be Christians. But as I grew older and rubbed shoulders with real Catholics in everyday life, it seemed clear to me that they were often as pious and "spirit-filled" as my other Christian friends, and it became equally clear that Protestants could be as nasty as anyone else. These experiences eventually influenced my reading of Scripture, as I turned again to the biblical text and discovered in it new resources for a more ecumenical understanding of the people of God. Thus, personal experience deeply impacted my sense of God, neighbor, Scripture, and tradition. And it did so, not by contradicting the voices of the Spirit, Scripture, and tradition, but rather by forcing me to perceive and understand their voices better.

Michael Polanyi has explained why experience is so important in our

---

20. Hence, I must respectfully disagree with Oden's claim that "Scripture and tradition are received, understood, and validated through personal experience, but not judged or arbitrated or censored by it." Thomas C. Oden, *Systematic Theology* (3 vols.; Peabody: Prince Press, 1998), 1.339.

pursuit of the truth. He pointed out that we always understand more about life than we can explicitly say. So when we turn to the voice of experience, we turn to a source of insight that runs deeper and is more detailed than the truths that we can speak and write about. The evidence of experience is therefore compelling, especially when it coheres with other sources of insight such as Scripture and tradition.[21] And precisely on account of this, when our full-orbed "gut-feel" comes to blows with our cognitive theological affirmations, this experiential evidence is a hint that our theological views may stand in need of refinement and modification. In pointing this out, I do not intend to suggest that experience is a sure-fire guide to the truth. Experience is a fallible voice that can and has led us far astray, so it must be informed by and weighed carefully against other sources of theological insight.[22] Nevertheless, where experience clearly conflicts with our beliefs about what is supposedly right and true, we must take its testimony seriously.

Although "experience" figures prominently in discussions of epistemology and hermeneutics, in systematic theology it is often subsumed into other matters, especially into discussions of the Spirit, of spiritual experience, and of natural theology. While there is nothing inherently mistaken about this, one result is that experience, in the broadest sense, is a much-neglected theme in some Christian accounts of theological reflection.[23] But admit it or not, our theology *always* drinks deeply from the well of experience.

IN SUM, WE DERIVE OUR THEOLOGY from the broken voices of Scripture, cosmos, tradition, and experience, and with the mysterious help of God's Spirit, who speaks through them. Good theology pursues the truth by listening to and coherently ordering all the important sources through which God speaks. May God help us to do this well.

---

21. See Oden, *Systematic Theology* 1.339.

22. For the practical application of experience to ethical reflection, see Richard B. Hays, *The Moral Vision of the New Testament* (San Francisco: HarperCollins, 1996), especially pp. 297-99 and 313-470.

23. Notable exceptions are the Wesleyan tradition (see Donald A. D. Thorsen, *The Wesleyan Quadrilateral: Scripture, Reason and Experience as a Model of Evangelical Theology* [Grand Rapids: Zondervan, 1990]) and the so-called "experiential-expressive" tradition described in George A. Lindbeck, *The Nature of Doctrine* (Philadelphia: Westminster, 1984), 30-45.

CHAPTER 12

Priorities for Theological Interpretation

Theological interpretation of Scripture cannot focus narrowly on the Bible itself but must address a wide range of issues and questions. My purpose in this chapter is to mention, almost in passing, several priorities that contemporary theorists now regard as important and to some extent neglected in the practice and theory of theological interpretation. The four subjects that I will consider are: mystery, personal wholeness, praxis, and mission.

Mystery

Modernism construes "reason" as a single, universal capacity shared by all people. Many postmodern theorists believe that this conception of reason has a dark side. Reason so defined, they say, readily yields the principle that "reasonable" people accept the truth and "unreasonable" people reject it. All too easily, this logic justifies the oppression and persecution of the "unreasonable" people who disagree with us.[1] This is the idea.

---

1. For the threat of rationalism in theology, see Delvin Brown, "Knowing the Mystery of God: Neville and Apophatic Thelogy," *American Journal of Theology and Philosophy* 18 (1997): 239-55. My sense is that Brown goes too far by resisting all theological truth assertions about God, but his practical concerns are laudable.

In many respect, I believe that this fear is well-founded. Danger lurks in the shadows of rationalism. If this is true, then intellectual and spiritual health requires that we respect the limits of human knowledge and rationality. We must learn how to embrace *mystery.*

As words go, "mystery" is itself a bit mysterious if one thinks about it much. We can speak of "investigative conundrums," such as a Sherlock Holmes who-done-it, of "extensive mysteries" that we cannot unravel because the data are simply unmanageable, of "dimensional mysteries" that we understand in some but not all dimensions, of "doxological mysteries" that inexplicably stir our affections (such as sunsets or thoughts of God), and of "religious mysteries" that we cannot resolve, such as the existence of evil.[2] The overlaps and connections between these types of mystery resist any simple typology. My main concern is to emphasize that theological inquiry requires a healthy respect for the limits of our human capacity to get at "the truth."

The church has always maintained that, in principle, neither revelation nor reason lead to anything like complete knowledge. Much remains mysterious, especially when it comes to theology. Chrysostom's famous essay "On the Incomprehensible Nature of God" is a classic explication of the point.[3] In spite of this ancient precedent, several scholars have pointed out that modern theology often leaves little room for mystery.[4] Modern theology tends to construe mystery in terms of deficiency rather than plenitude, so that anything we do not understand — such as the Holy Trinity — becomes a problem to be solved rather than a perpetual mystery to be embraced and enjoyed.[5] As a result, modern theologians have often demanded and proffered ready answers for many or all of theology's

2. For a typology of mystery, see Steven D. Boyer, "The Logic of Mystery," *RelStud* 43 (2007): 89-102; Bernard J. Verkamp, *Senses of Mystery: Religious and Non-Religious* (Scranton, PA: University of Scranton, 1997).

3. John Chrysostom, *On The Incomprehensible Nature of God*, tr. Paul W. Harkins (Fathers of the Church 34; Washington, DC: Catholic University of America, 1984).

4. Andrew Louth, *Discerning the Mystery: An Essay on the Nature of Theology* (Oxford: Clarendon, 1990); William C. Placher, *The Domestication of Transcendence* (Louisville: Westminster John Knox, 1996).

5. Karl Rahner, "The Concept of Mystery in Catholic Theology," in *Theological Investigations* 5/4, tr. K. Smith (Baltimore: Helicon; London: Darton, Longman & Todd, 1974), 36-73.

perplexing questions. Why do people suffer? How does divine sovereignty relate to human freedom? What is the nature of the Trinity? How was the Bible "inspired"? The result is what one scholar has called the "domestication of transcendence," in that our theology begins to rigidly define who God is and what he can (and cannot) do. One theological domino quickly hits another, in a cascade that spawns all sorts of inflexible but misplaced assumptions about Christian theory and practice.[6]

The problem in these cases is certainly *not* that we are trying to say something rational, logical, and systematic about theology. We can and should say something about it, doing so on the basis of rationales informed by Scripture and other sources of insight. Rather, the problem is that modern theology sometimes tries to do too much with too little. We imagine that Scripture and reason answer questions that they simply do not answer or, at least, do not answer as well as we think. This overreaching rationalism impairs our theological reflection. Theology necessarily becomes reductionistic: too simple to do justice to God and his work in the world. Our conceptions of God are corrupted more and more by errant deductions about what "must" be theologically true. Also, because we tend to lose a sense of God's transcendence and holiness in this scenario, divine uniqueness deteriorates into mere rhetoric as "mystery" disappears from the indexes of our systematic theologies. As Durkheim famously quipped, we create God in our own image.[7]

Mystery is not a matter of theology only. It inheres in every interpretive judgment because our grasp of the truth is always analogical and practical rather than complete. So in matters of science, literature, and ethics, no less than in theology, the door of inquiry must remain ajar to the possibility of better insight. To be sure, granting mystery a prominent place in our reflection will not entirely prevent us from pushing reason beyond its limits, nor will it forestall all error. But we will be less prone to err in this way if we leave ample room for mystery.

Of course, it is quite true that appeals to mystery can be misplaced. Far too often Christians have used mystery as an "escape hatch" to save

---

6. Placher, *The Domestication of Transcendence.*

7. Emile Durkheim, *The Elementary Forms of the Religious Life,* tr. K. E. Fields (New York: Free Press, 1995). The book was originally published in French in 1912.

their theology when it faces troubling evidence. I am reminded, by way of example, of one fundamentalist response to the evidence for evolution and an old earth:

> At the end of the day, if I'm asked the question "why does the universe look so old?" I'm simply left with the reality that the universe is telling the story of the glory of God. Why does it look so old? Well that, in terms of any more elaborate answer, is known only to the Ancient of Days. And that is where we are left.[8]

Rather than admit that the universe really is as ancient as the evidence suggests, this theologian — who believes in young earth creationism — simply discards the strange scientific evidence as a "mystery." As this example illustrates, we should by all means avoid frivolous appeals to mystery that too quickly cede the ground of evidence to confessions of ignorance. When it comes to the age of the cosmos, "red-shift" and the decay of radioactive isotopes are as much God's voice as Genesis 1.

Personal Wholeness

Our theme at this point is "wholeness," by which I refer to our spiritual, emotional, and psychological health. It is beyond the scope of the present discussion to advance a detailed vision for what personal wholeness looks like, but I will say this. If we wish to hear and follow the Spirit's voice in a life of love for God and neighbor, this end is best pursued by those who seek and have experienced some measure of healing from this broken world. For I cannot easily hear Scripture say "God loves you" if my experience in life has caused me to unconsciously doubt or hate God. Similarly, I cannot really look after my neighbor's welfare if I live in constant but unexamined anxiety about my own situation and future. *Spiritual formation* is the aspect of theology under consideration here. How do we become integrated individuals who live in vital, loving relationships with God and our neighbors?

---

8. Albert C. Mohler, "Why Does the Universe Look So Old?" http://www.biologos.org/resources/albert-mohler-why-does-the-universe-look-so-old.

Others have written ably on this subject, so I will offer only the briefest sketch of some important elements.[9] Foremost, we must keep in mind that we will not be whole on this side of eternity. As Augustine pointed out long ago, we are on a *journey,* in the process of becoming whole:

> Let us look upon this purification as a kind of journey or voyage to our native land. For it is not by change of place that we come nearer to Him who is in every place, but by the cultivation of pure desires and virtuous habits.[10]

Augustine did not create the "journey" metaphor. He was undoubtedly influenced by biblical language, especially from the Old Testament, which often uses words like "path," "way," and "walk" to describe the life of religious piety. As Augustine goes on to say, those are most healthy who travel this spiritual path:

> For a man is never in so good a state as when his whole life is a journey towards the unchangeable life, and his affections are entirely fixed upon that.[11]

This applies even to Jesus himself, who "learned obedience through what he suffered" and became "perfect" in the process (Heb 5:8). Life is a journey where we learn to "walk as Jesus did" (1 John 2:6). It comes as no surprise, then, that early Christians were referred to as those who belonged to "the Way" (Acts 9:2).

Scripture teaches that the journey to wholeness is not traveled alone. Genesis provides the first hint in this direction when it tells us that Adam was *alone* in God's garden. We were designed to pursue and experience wholeness through healthy relationships with God *and* others. Mutuality stands at the center of human formation because, as so many have emphasized over the years, we simply cannot know ourselves apart from the

9. I would suggest anything written by Henri J. M. Nouwen, including especially *The Return of the Prodigal Son: A Meditation on Fathers, Brothers, and Sons* (New York: Doubleday, 1992).

10. *On Christian Doctrine* 12.10 (NPNF1 2.525).

11. *On Christian Doctrine* 22.21 (NPNF1 2.527).

help of God and our community. As Colin Gunton expressed it, someone else must provide "the mirrors in which we may see ourselves as we are."[12]

Ideally, we are progressively equipped to travel the road to wholeness from birth to the grave by nurturing parents, loving families, close friends, those in the church, and pastors, teachers, and spiritual mentors who "equip" us for love and good deeds. In some cases, however, the psychological and spiritual damage from our fallen situation has taken a terrible toll and makes all of this very difficult. Perhaps our biochemistry makes us anxious or psychotic. Or perhaps abuse of some sort or other has made it hard to trust anyone. Or perhaps the death of a loved one has robbed us of hope and joy. In these cases and many others, wisdom is needed to work through the difficulties as we pursue healing. We are fortunate in our day to know a great deal about psychological function and to have at our disposal numerous therapeutic strategies that can lead to better health. We also have medications that assist with organically-driven pathologies. We should avail ourselves of these resources and be thankful that God has made them available.

I would caution, in passing, that psychological therapies based on a fundamentalist view of Scripture — sometimes called "biblical counseling" — can be very damaging to those who are hurting.[13] As the Pontifical Biblical Commission expressed it,

> The fundamentalist approach is dangerous, for it is attractive to people who look to the Bible for ready answers to the problems of life. It can deceive these people, offering them interpretations that are pious but illusory, instead of telling them that the Bible does not necessarily contain an immediate answer to each and every problem. . . . It injects into

---

12. Colin E. Gunton, *Christ and Creation* (Grand Rapids: Eerdmans, 1992), 72. Many have written on these themes, though with quite varied notions of what it means to "know God" or other persons. For my own part, I would suggest the following: Lesslie Newbigin, "Knowing God," in *Proper Confidence: Faith, Doubt, and Certainty in Christian Discipleship* (Grand Rapids: Eerdmans, 1995), 45-64; Paul Ricoeur, *Oneself as Another* (Chicago: University of Chicago Press, 1992); Jens Zimmerman, *Recovering Theological Hermeneutics: An Incarnational-Trinitarian Theory of Interpretation* (Grand Rapids: Baker, 2004).

13. Here I would commend to conservative readers the new book by Everett L. Worthington, *Coming to Peace with Psychology* (Downers Grove: InterVarsity, 2010).

life a false certitude, for it unwittingly confuses the divine substance of the biblical message with what are in fact its human limitations.[14]

Though Scripture contributes significantly to a fuller understanding of human psychology and wholeness, it is not an adequate basis for a good understanding of psychological function. Fundamentalist biblicism, to its own detriment, tends to believe that Scripture is a self-help book with answers for all of our problems.[15] But Scripture, and people, are far more complicated than fundamentalists sometimes suppose.

At any rate, to return to our main theme, we can easily read the Bible every day and never notice the way that spiritual blindness, psychological damage, and emotional handicap warp our reading of Scripture and our theological rationale. Insofar as it is possible and feasible, we should pursue the spiritual, emotional, and psychological wholeness that makes us healthy people who can better hear and live out the word of God.

Praxis: Performing the Scriptures

Nicholas Lash has pointed out that Scripture is like Shakespeare's *King Lear*.[16] Though it is quite possible to merely read and understand Scripture's discourse, the text has not reached its *telos* — its proper end — until readers "perform" it by living it out. If this is right, and if it is true that the chief end of humanity is to love God and neighbor, then we should not lose sight of the fact that all we have been discussing here — the Bible, theology, culture, philosophy, conscience, literary genre, ancient languages and contexts — properly stands in the service of God's redemptive plan to create a church that lives out the gospel of love. To interpret Scripture correctly is to be "seized by truth" and "captive to the Word of God."[17]

14. D. P. Béchard, *The Scripture Documents: An Anthology of Official Catholic Teachings* (Collegeville, MN: Liturgial, 2002), 274-75.

15. For a thoughtful analysis and critique of this perspective, see Christian Smith, *The Impossibility of Evangelical Biblicism* (Grand Rapids, MI: Brazos, forthcoming).

16. Nicholas Lash, "Performing the Scriptures," in his *Theology on the Way to Emmaus* (London: SCM Press, 1986), 37-46.

17. Here reflecting the titles of two recent books, Joel B. Green, *Seized by Truth: Reading*

In saying this, I do not intend just to repeat the old Christian adage about "walking the talk" and similar aphorisms that admonish us to live out God's commands as we understand them. I mean to say as well that, in a very *theoretical* sense, I have not interpreted Scripture adequately until I have acted on what God has said. An adequate understanding of the truth is always an embodied truth. It always results in a correspondingly wiser and healthier way of life that respects God and neighbor. We delude ourselves when we are only hearers, and not doers, of God's word (Jas 1:22).

Precisely because praxis takes our theology into the trenches of real life, it also serves a vital role in our theological reflection. Theology that works well in actual practice is more likely to be healthy theology, whereas failure raises the possibility that our theology is wanting in some respects. As an example, some early Christians actually believed that sins committed after baptism could not be forgiven, resulting in a rather awkward theological predicament because all Christians *do* sin after conversion.[18] The obvious tension between doctrine and lived experience ultimately revealed that this theology simply could not be right. Of course good theology is in its own way difficult to live out, so "failure" does not provide a failsafe theological litmus test. But the point remains important: good theological judgments foster success in serving God's cause, and poor judgments do not.

Christian praxis is the fundamental goal of Scripture and hence is the context in which we hone our theological tools, both theoretical and practical. Insofar as we neglect ongoing reflection on praxis, we do so to our theological detriment.

A Missional Hermeneutic

Stimulated especially by texts that describe Christ as reconciling *"all things"* to God (e.g., Col 1:20), many contemporary theologians have em-

---

the Bible as Scripture (Nashville: Abingdon, 2007), and Miroslav Volf, *Captive to the Word of God: Engaging the Scriptures for Contemporary Theological Reflection* (Grand Rapids: Eerdmans, 2010).

18. Everett Ferguson, *Baptism in the Early Church: History, Theology, and Liturgy in the First Five Centuries* (Grand Rapids: Eerdmans, 2009), 214-20.

phasized the importance of *mission* in our theological reflection on Scripture.[19] The stress is laid not merely on Christian missionary work *per se* but rather more broadly on the *missio Dei*, the "mission of God" to redeem the whole created order through the work of Christ and his church. Missional theology is concerned not only for individuals but also for the social and political order, the welfare of animals, stewardship of the environment, and anything else pertaining to God's redemptive work. Care for the environment has become a particularly important emphasis in recent years on the assumption that the body of Christ is responsible for preserving nature as an expression of God's glory and as the home of humanity and all living things.

Some Christians have suggested that missional thinkers neglect the church's responsibility to present the gospel to the world, that they hug trees and save whales rather than lead people to Jesus. While it is sometimes true that missional theology can be out of balance, in principle this is a misunderstanding of the intent. Missional theology construes the church's redemptive work more broadly than traditional evangelism does, largely on the assumption that everything done in the name of Christ should provide a suitable witness for unbelievers. We can do evangelism *and* recycle.

Missional thinking has important implications for biblical interpretation. Here I will mention two. First, Bonhoeffer has alerted us to the fact that we must live our lives in the *penultimate* — the things *before* the last — rather than in the *ultimate* world to come.[20] By this he meant that we live not as if we are already in heaven but, rather, as people in a struggle against evil and pain in a broken world still longing for redemption. Jesus did not greet the death of Lazarus with a celebration of his friend's salvation. He wept because his friend was dead. In a similar way, we must resist the temptation to live as if Christ's victory over sin has liberated us from the struggle against sin. Biblical interpretation and theological praxis must be fit for our mission in a broken world. We must live the penultimate for the sake of the ultimate.

19. Michael J. Gorman, *Elements of Biblical Exegesis* (rev. ed.; Peabody, MA: Hendrickson, 2009), 155-58; cf. Karl Barth, *The Humanity of God* (Richmond: John Knox, 1960), 61-62.

20. Dietrich Bonhoeffer, *Ethics*, tr. N. H. Smith (New York: Macmillan, 1955), 120-85.

Second, our mission in the world implies that our reading of Scripture should not occasion embarrassment before an unbelieving world. Aquinas expressed it this way in his *Summa Theologica:* "one should adhere to a particular explanation [of Scripture] only in such measure as to be ready to abandon it, if it be proved with certainty to be false; lest Holy Scripture be exposed to the ridicule of unbelievers, and obstacles be placed to their believing."[21] Augustine expressed a similar concern in his commentary on Genesis: "it is a disgraceful and dangerous thing for an infidel to hear a Christian, presumably giving the meaning of Holy Scripture, talking nonsense on these [cosmological] topics, and we should take all means to prevent such an embarrassing situation, in which people show up vast ignorance in a Christian and laugh it to scorn."[22] Neither Augustine nor Aquinas, nor I in following them, wish to evade or ignore God's word in Scripture. There certainly are things that God has said in his word that are stumbling blocks to unbelievers, most notably the Christian claim that Jesus Christ is the one and only savior of the cosmos. Nevertheless, I agree with Augustine and Aquinas that we should pause before we advance an interpretation of Scripture that makes God out as saying things that are an embarrassment to the faith. Often enough, these interpretations are an embarrassment precisely because they are wrong.

I would part ways with Augustine and Aquinas mainly with respect to their interpretive strategy. Whereas the fathers happily appealed to allegory or some other "fuller sense" of Scripture to avoid embarrassment, I believe that we live in a time when the allegories themselves occasion astonishment and ridicule. A better theological path will simply admit that the biblical authors were flesh-and-blood human beings whose fallible words are used by God in his redemptive work. These biblical authors may sometimes have said things that embarrass us, but God says no such things.

---

21. 1, q. 68, in *Summa Theologica* (5 vols.; Allen, TX: Christian Classics, 1981), 1.338.

22. Augustine, *The Literal Meaning of Genesis*, tr. J. H. Taylor (2 vols.; New York: Paulist Press, 1982), 1.42-43.

CHAPTER 13

Validity and Biblical Interpretation

According to the canons of modern epistemology, "valid" readings of Scripture are those that successfully recover the true intentions of the biblical authors. I have already pointed out that this uncomplicated conception of validity is problematic in various ways. First, interpretation involves much more than the author's intention, so there are many things that one can get right (or wrong) in the quest to understanding how Scripture contributes to and informs good theology. Secondly, our grasp of the author's meaning is always analogical and at best useful for particular purposes or questions; it does not yield anything like a complete understanding of the author's intentions, much less of their implications. Third, and perhaps most importantly, there is simply no way to insure that one's grasp of an author's intention is right. We can and should do our best to understand Scripture and to reach convictions about what it says and how it directs us to live as followers of Christ, but to demand something more — such as the incorrigible certainty that our interpretation is right — only leads us again into the trap that snared our first parents and Job's friends.

Now, having said this, surely it is the case that some interpretations are better than others and that, practically speaking, we must make judgments about which interpretations are good and right as opposed to wrong or poor. How can we say with a straight face, in a postmodern era, that some readings are valid and others are not? This is the question that I will try to address here, though I forewarn readers that these territories are fraught with philosophical difficulties and complexities on many levels. I have no comprehensive theory to offer but only some basic observations that I hope will be useful as we consider the perennial question of validity in biblical interpretation.

Warrant and Validity: The God's-Eye View

I wish to begin by introducing two interrelated but conceptually different terms, *warrant* and *validity*. The first term, warrant, refers to whether one has good reasons for an interpretation of Scripture.[1] As an example, it is fairly easy to accept that Christians living in the first century had good reasons for thinking that there were "waters above the heavens." This was based on a straightforward reading of Genesis 1 and did not contradict the science as they understood it. So their belief about these waters was "warranted." Modern scientific knowledge does not change this in the slightest because "warranted" interpretations are not necessarily right. Rather, warranted interpretations are reasonable and sensible for those who hold them.

Validity is the term that I use with reference to whether an interpretation is right. Put more elegantly, valid interpretations are "correct," "right," "healthy," and "wise," whereas invalid interpretations are "incorrect," "wrong," "evil," and "foolish." I have used a constellation of adjectives here because, as we shall see, the best adjective varies with the interpretive context. To return to our example from Genesis in the previous paragraph, we could say that the ancient belief in heavenly waters was warranted (being embraced for good reasons) but also invalid (because these waters do not exist).

Ideally our interpretations will be both warranted and valid. But who will finally decide whether an interpretation clears this bar? From a theistic point of view, it seems to me that only one perspective offers a faultless

---

1. For those versed in epistemology, I employ "warrant" in a way that conceptually includes both "internalistic justification" and "externalistic warrant." For an accessible introductory discussion of these terms and their subtleties, see W. Jay Wood, *Epistemology: Becoming Intellectually Virtuous* (Downers Grove, IL: InterVarsity, 1998).

evaluation of our interpretations: God's perspective. I am obviously in no position to discuss this "God's-eye" view in any great detail, but it seems to me that a tentative sketch of the God's-eye view, based on Scripture and native insight, will help us think about how we, as human beings, should make our judgments about warrant and validity.

Foremost, I think that it goes without saying that God does not judge our interpretations by the standards of his own knowledge. God judges the warrant and validity of our interpretations by criteria more suited to our human limitations. This conclusion is rationally sensible and also explicitly biblical. The Apostle Paul's speech in Acts 17 immediately comes to mind.[2] Here Paul explained to his Greek audience that God had overlooked their past idolatries because these were committed in ignorance. Thus he acknowledges that, to some extent, the lost Greeks had warrant for their errant religious practices, particularly for their worship of an "unknown God" (Acts 17:23). The underlying principle of Paul's theology is aptly expressed in Psalm 103:

> Bless the LORD, O my soul, and forget not all his benefits, who forgives all your iniquity, who heals all your diseases, who redeems your life from the pit.... The LORD is merciful and gracious, slow to anger and abounding in steadfast love. He will not always chide, nor will he keep his anger forever. He does not deal with us according to our sins, nor requite us according to our iniquities.... As a father pities his children, so the LORD pities those who fear him. For he knows our frame; he remembers that we are dust.

As this important text points out, divine judgment gives ground not only to our finite perspectives but also, to some extent, to our fallen, fleshly frames. Jesus himself applied this principle in his memorable words, "Father, forgive them, for they do not know what they are doing."

I am not suggesting at all that God makes light of our sin or that no instances exist in which we really are culpable and guilty for things that we have done. But God's judgment in these matters seems to be on a "sliding

2. Some scholars believe that the portrait of Paul in Acts is more fictional than historical, but this has no bearing on my immediate purpose.

scale" that evades a simple good vs. evil distinction. As Jesus put it in Luke's Gospel, "[The] servant who knew his master's will, but did not make ready or act according to his will, shall receive a severe beating. But he who did not know, and did what deserved a beating, shall receive a light beating. Every one to whom much is given, of him will much be required" (Luke 12:47-48).

Another hint about God's perspective on warrant and validity is provided in the little story told by Jesus about the Good Samaritan. Particularly interesting and relevant is that Jesus sided with the heretic Samaritan, who loved his suffering neighbor, over the orthodox Jews who did not.[3] The point is that God, in making his judgments about us, is more concerned about our moral and ethical formation, and its resulting praxis, than about doctrinal and theological consistency. This kind of judgment is sensible because human beings are not wholly consistent when it comes to life and theology. Rationally sensible theology does not always lead to right living, nor does theological confusion necessarily lead to vice. So, contrary to the western philosophical notion that validity is about good rational arguments, the Christian tradition would hold that intellectual arguments are important but in some ways secondary when it comes to validity. The actual life that we live in response to Scripture is the most important mark of valid biblical interpretation.

But to return to my earlier and very important point, Scripture teaches that God is the final arbiter of validity. Paul implies this in 1 Corinthians 4. "My conscience is clear" he wrote, "but that does not make me innocent. It is the Lord who judges me" (1 Cor 4:3-4). While Paul, like all of us, had a responsibility to pursue and draw valid conclusions and inferences about Scripture, theology, and his personal life, he was well aware that these human judgments — however important and useful — are not the final word on interpretation. In this respect, I think that the pragmatic

---

3. As we learn from early Jewish and Christian sources, the Samaritans did not accept the entire Old Testament canon (they used only the Pentateuch) nor did they believe in the afterlife. So the paradox of the story is greater than often noticed, since the basic point is that the Samaritan, who did not believe in eternal life, would receive it, whereas the Jews who believed in eternal life would not. For the early Jewish and Christian sources, see Origen, homily 25 in *Homilies on Numbers*, tr. T. P. Scheck (Downers Grove, IL: InterVarsity, 2009), 154; R. J. Coggins, *Samaritans and Jews* (Atlanta: John Knox, 1975), 139-40.

antirealist philosopher Richard Rorty was at least partly if not wholly right when he said that, apart from a final divine tribunal on the Truth convened by God, there is no such thing as *Truth*.

Ultimately, God must decide whether and to what extent our interpretive judgments are warranted and valid. To notice and appreciate this is to recognize God's authority and also (at least for me) to gain a degree of pastoral comfort, knowing that our efforts as biblical interpreters will be judged by the God of love and grace. At the same time, this affirmation brings us full circle back to the hermeneutical challenge before us: living as we do on this side of eternity, we simply do not have foolproof access to God's divine perspective on warrant and validity. We make these judgments for ourselves (though not necessarily *by* ourselves) and, according to Scripture, will be held accountable for these judgments, especially if we are Christian teachers (see Jas 3:1).

Warrant

Let us now consider how we, as human beings, should make judgments about warrant and validity. I suggest that we begin by considering the benefits of the first term, warrant.

If warranted readings can be wrong, of what conceptual benefit can "warrant" possibly be? Warrant is the path to valid interpretation. Though we lack the power to insure that our interpretations of Scripture are right, we *do* have the capacity to insure that our interpretive efforts are wise and serious. By definition, warranted interpretations are "good-faith" attempts to read Scripture well. This observation has spawned a new movement in philosophy call "virtue epistemology." Its advocates advise us to pay less attention to "getting it right" and more attention to becoming the kinds of person who get things right. Positive epistemic virtues include wisdom, foresight, studiousness, industriousness, prudence, intellectual honesty, and discernment. Epistemic vices include folly, obtuseness, laziness, superficiality, gullibility, closed-mindedness, dishonesty, and willful naiveté.[4] Good interpreters seek to incarnate the

4. Wood, *Epistemology*.

virtues and avoid the vices. We discover our epistemic weaknesses most readily when we realize that our interpretations are wrong. In these cases, one of our first priorities is to consider whether particular epistemic vices have caused us to get at faulty answers. Thus, just as warrant is the path to valid interpretation, so invalid interpretation is a clue that exposes unwarranted interpretation.

Warrant has other benefits as well. It reminds us that people can hold differing and even mistaken opinions for good reasons. When we are aware of this, we are more likely to engage our opponents in theological debates about biblical interpretation with attitudes of love, peace, patience, and kindness rather than anger, arrogance, irritation, and divisiveness. Another benefit of warrant is that it assumes the human capacity for interpretation is pretty good, so that most of our warranted interpretations are at least partly right. If we therefore assume that other interpretations of Scripture probably bring something useful to the table of theological debate and discussion, this ought to help us be "quick to listen" and "slow to speak and become angry" (Jas 1:19). Warrant also reminds us that our own interpretations, however sensible and obvious they may seem to us at the time, could well turn out to be wrong.

Validity

All interpretations are not created equal. As I pointed out earlier, I use the term *validity* with reference to whether interpretations are best described as good, right, and wise *(valid)* or poor, wrong, and foolish *(invalid)*. Judgments about validity (like judgments about warrant) are contextual. Let us take Eugene H. Merrill's article on the biblical genocide texts as an example.[5] In it Merrill concludes that God really did command the Israelites to violently slaughter the Canaanites because God wanted to give their land to Israel and because the Canaanites represented a spiritual threat to Israel. If we judge this reading of Scripture by the canons of biblical scholarship, which maintain that a good reading of the Bible ascertains the bibli-

---

5. Eugene H. Merrill, "The Case for Moderate Discontinuity," in Stanley N. Gundry, ed., *Show Them No Mercy* (Grand Rapids: Zondervan, 2003), 63-109.

cal author's viewpoint, then we might well conclude that Merrill's reading of Deuteronomy is essentially *valid* because the ancient biblical author probably did believe that God was in the business of slaughtering Canaanites. Merrill has it right.

But let us suppose, for the sake of discussion, that we are not interested merely in the question of whether Merrill has understood the Bible's human author. Let us also ask whether Merrill has understood the divine discourse of Scripture by examining what he does with the text theologically. Here, for example, is one of his theological comments:

> The issue, then, cannot be whether or not genocide is intrinsically good or evil — its sanction by a holy God settles that question. Rather, the issue has to do with the purpose of genocide, its initiator, and the particular circumstances of its application.[6]

In contrast to our former judgment, now I think we must judge Merrill's reading to be *invalid*. For a full-orbed, biblically informed portrait of God's character simply will not permit us to conclude that God, under any circumstances, would order his people to systematically terrorize and slaughter an ethnic group — including even innocent children — because of its religious and cultural identity. Fortunately, Merrill describes the Canaanite genocide as a "unique situation" that Christians should not repeat, but much of the theological damage has already been done to his portrait of God.

This example illustrates the complexity of judgments about validity. Not only are these judgments contextual (in that they depend on interpretive situations and goals), but they are also multilayered because even invalid interpretations, such as this one, include some degree of "valid" understanding. In effect, to say that a reading of Scripture is valid or invalid is shorthand for saying that, *overall*, the reading is "good," "right," "wise," and "useful" (valid) as opposed to "poor," "wrong," "foolish," and "unhelpful" (invalid). In this case I would say that, on the whole, Merrill's reading of Scripture as divine discourse is *invalid* because it is poor, generally unhelpful, and in the wrong hands perhaps a little dangerous.

6. Merrill, "Case," 93.

148

Readers from Merrill's own religious community would undoubtedly offer a different evaluation of his article and its validity. I will consider the role of "community" in interpretation below.

Surplus of Meaning and Validity

Most recent discussions of theological interpretation accentuate the Bible's "surplus of meaning."[7] By this scholars imply that texts do not have one determinate meaning — such as the author's meaning, for example — but rather multiple legitimate meanings. Priority is given to multiple meanings out of deference to God, whose "intentions" could never be subsumed entirely by any single human meaning, and also out of deference to the inevitable fact that Christians read the text differently — and it simply cannot be the case that one reader has it right and everyone else is wrong. Scholars often support this pluralistic construal of biblical interpretation by an appeal to the Christian tradition, which has long held that a single biblical text might have several legitimate meanings. The parade example is the traditional "fourfold sense" of Scripture advocated by the early fathers, according to which Scripture bears literal, allegorical, tropological, and anagogical levels of meanings.[8] Some scholars argue that this "fourfold" sense not only justifies multiple meanings but also points us in an entirely different hermeneutical direction; we should replace modern critical approaches with a "return to allegory."[9] Again, the obvious motivation is to make room for a wide range of "valid" interpretations of Scripture.

7. A. K. M. Adam, *Faithful Interpretation* (Minneapolis: Fortress, 2006), 81-103; Ellen F. Davis and Richard B. Hays, eds., *The Art of Reading Scripture* (Grand Rapids: Eerdmans, 2003), 2-3; Stephen E. Fowl, *Engaging Scripture: A Model for Theological Interpretation* (Malden, MA: Blackwell, 1998), 32-61.

8. As we might expect, this "fourfold" system was construed in different ways in antiquity. According to the nomenclature above, "allegorical" meanings are Christological, "tropological" meanings are moral and ethical, and "anagogical" meanings are eschatological.

9. The classic essay is David C. Steinmetz, "The Superiority of Pre-Critical Exegesis," *ThTo* 37 (1980): 27-38. For a recent and more detailed discussion, see J. Todd. Billings, *The Word of God for the People of God: An Entryway to the Theological Interpretation of Scripture* (Grand Rapids: Eerdmans, 2010), 149-94.

The "multi-voiced" approach to Scripture obviously raises questions about how validity should be understood. If many different readings are valid, in what sense can we say that some are valid and some are not? Scholars who advocate multi-voiced readings usually give two answers to this question. First, they suppose that the biblical text itself "limits" the range of interpretive options for readers, so that there is a natural boundary on what counts as valid. And, second, they argue that the reader's community of faith places fairly rigid limits on what counts as a valid interpretation. If I try to read Scripture in a way that denies the divinity of Jesus, for instance, my faith community will confront that reading, both to set me straight and to prevent my reading from becoming accepted and normative within the church.

Contemporary theological interpreters offer other explications of validity, but these two things — text and community — seem to provide the primary criteria for securing validity.

I quite agree that Scripture has multiple valid meanings and that the text and community facilitate judgments about validity. Yet it seems to me that there are problems with this construal of validity as it stands, problems that we can resolve somewhat better by applying the benefits of Practical Realism to our understanding of theological interpretation.

Rather than turn to mysterious allegorical meanings to make room for Scripture's multi-voiced character, let us turn instead to Practical Realism's observation that all textual interpretations are analogies that approach the text from a different vantage point and so get at the text's meaning in different ways. Hence, even if we embrace the text as the historically-conditioned discourse of an ancient human author and attend closely to that author's motives and intentions, this still leaves room for a wide range of valid readings. To illustrate the point, let us consider an excerpt from Paul's letter to the Philippians:

> Have this mind among yourselves, which is yours in Christ Jesus, who, though he was in the form of God, did not count equality with God a thing to be grasped, but emptied himself, taking the form of a servant, being born in the likeness of men. And being found in human form he humbled himself and became obedient unto death, even death on a cross. Therefore God has highly exalted him and bestowed on him the name

which is above every name, that at the name of Jesus every knee should bow, in heaven and on earth and under the earth, and every tongue confess that Jesus Christ is Lord, to the glory of God the Father. (Phil 2:5-11)

If we engage this text as the words of an ancient Christian apostle, what readings might count as valid? One reader might say, "Here we see an emphasis on the divinity of Jesus — that he is truly God but laid aside certain prerogatives of his divinity in order to take on human flesh." Another reader might say, "Here we see a profound image of the humanity of Jesus — that he was actually born as a flesh-and-blood human being who suffered on the cross." Or "Here we see a hint of the universal scope of what Christ has accomplished, in that *every* knee in the created and cosmic order will bow to his Lordship." Or "Here Paul labors to inspire the Philippians to be less selfish and more willing to live with an eye on serving others." Or "Church and business administrators would do well to obey Paul by emulating Jesus in their leadership styles." Or "This text suggests that the Philippians had some significant problems getting along with each other." Or "I think that God is challenging me to be more selfless in service to my family and church." Or "This is an aesthetically beautiful piece of early Christian poetry." Or "Here we see that Paul believed in a three-tiered cosmos, with heaven above the earth and Hades below."

Although these readings of the text reflect quite varied interests and obviously engage the text in very different ways, I would judge that each is (or could be) valid insofar as it "gets at" something that is true of God, Christ, Paul, humanity, the Philippians, the Greek language, or the reader. Some of these readings are closely tied to Paul's intentions and some are not, but none of them is wholly foreign to his ancient discourse as preserved in Scripture. My point is that one does not need allegorical or tropological readings to make room for multiple legitimate readings of Scripture that address important theological issues and bring them to bear on modern thought and practice. Moreover, this broad approach to interpretation provides a philosophical explanation for the interpretive success in the ancient allegories. Consider Augustine's reading of Psalm 137 as an example. When the Psalmist ostensibly praises God as one who smashes Babylonian infants against the rocks, Augustine tells us that this is an allegory in which God destroys "evil desires at their birth."[10] As a Practical Realist and biblical scholar, I would judge that Augustine missed the intention of the Bible's human author but got something profoundly right about the divine author. For the God revealed in Jesus Christ would not smash babies against rocks.

Practical Realism raises an expectation that interpreters from different communities and cultures will offer different but nonetheless truthful and useful readings of the same text. Each reading is an analogy that "gets it right" in a particular but limited way. If this observation is taken seriously, the theoretical posture of Practical Realism should foster in us a corresponding posture of respect for other readings of Scripture. We will assume that each reading of Scripture contributes in some way to a fuller, more complete understanding of good theology and healthy Christian living. This being so, our commitment to Practical Realism — as a theologically informed description of the human situation — will direct our attention, in the first instance, to what other readings *bring* to the table before we engage in constructive criticism. The proper goal of interpretation is to understand and benefit from many human perspectives rather than endlessly debate their differences.

Community and Validity

My discussion so far appears to emphasize the individual's role in judgments of validity and warrant, but I certainly do not envision these judgments as mere exercises in individual preference. As I have already mentioned, one common approach to validity emphasizes the role of community in establishing validity. According to this logic, our readings of Scripture, and our theological conclusions, are validated by communal assent.[11] If I am tempted on the basis of 1 Cor 14:34 to conclude wrongly that women should literally "keep silent in the church," Christians in my immediate community will challenge my reading and in doing so prevent

---

10. *Commentary on Psalm 137* (NPNF1 8.630-32).

11. The classic essay is Edgar V. McKnight, "A Literary-Oriented Biblical Criticism," in *The Bible and the Reader: An Introduction to Literary Criticism* (Minneapolis: Fortress, 1985). More recently, see Adam, *Faithful Interpretation*; Fowl, *Engaging Scripture*.

it from becoming an accepted theological norm; they may also push me (either explicitly or implicitly) to alter my view so that my reading of Scripture conforms more closely to the actual judgments and practices of the community.

Community-based validity usually emphasizes not only the role of the immediate Christian community but also the importance of church tradition in general. When we appeal to "creedal orthodoxy" as a proper basis for biblical interpretation, for example, we are acknowledging the fundamental role that the Christian community "writ large" plays in our theological interpretation of Scripture. The potential resources from this ecumenical community are vast because there are so many major branches and denominations in Christendom. Interpreters of Scripture will have to make wise choices about the resources they should consider when they read the Bible theologically.

Christian communities also exert a tacit, unconscious influence on interpretation by rendering otiose some readings of Scripture that might otherwise seem possible. So, for instance, most Christians are unlikely to consider the possibility that we should predict the future by observing an arrow's flight, as Elisha does in 2 Kgs 13:17. The theological priorities of our respective Christian communities simply preclude this option. Tacit pressure to conform to community norms is very strong because our associations and affections, indeed our very lives, are closely tied to community and tradition. When it comes to interpretation this is a blessing but also, in some cases, a curse. Community is a blessing because it Christianly shapes my soul and provides a communal location for experiencing God's grace. It becomes a curse, however, if I begin to sacrifice the truth for the sake of preserving my place in the community. More often than we would like to admit, liberal and conservative Christians ape the party-line when they know or suspect that it lacks nuance and sensitivity. Serious theology must challenge the status quo when the community is wrong about important things.

Some theologians believe that interpretive confusion and theological debate can be resolved by simple appeals to the authority of the Christian community. This is especially common in Catholic and Eastern Orthodox circles, where church authorities hold sway over theology and biblical interpretation, but the idea shows up in some Protestant circles as well. It seems to me that this straightforward appeal to church authority faces at

SACRED WORD, BROKEN WORD

least three basic problems. First, as I have just pointed out, church tradition can be wrong. Second, the voice of "the church" is only workable as a final solution if one has already made an ecclesiological decision to submit to the authority of one and only one church hierarchy.[12] But if one takes a more ecumenical posture that recognizes the legitimacy of different and sometimes conflicting Christian traditions, this one-stop solution will not work as a final solution. Theology in a diverse church requires that we decide which community, or communities, speak to us with the greatest authority, and we must also decide how that communal authority figures in our theological reflection. Third, we should note the important observation of Pope Pius XII that "there are but few [biblical] texts whose sense has been defined by the authority of the church."[13] In other words, most of what we do in biblical interpretation is untouched, or only lightly touched, by the creedal and catechetical judgments of church tradition. So regardless of our church tradition, it turns out our judgments about validity cannot depend on the authority of the church in most cases.

Neither community-based nor individually-focused approaches to warrant and validity solve all our interpretive problems. Christians are responsible both to the views of the church community and also to the dictates of their own understanding and conscience, as Paul so often points out.[14] There is simply no way this side of heaven for human beings to escape the complexity of the hermeneutical circle and its many and varied elements.

Engaging Invalid and Unwarranted Interpretations

We are confronted at times by biblical interpretations and theological conclusions that we judge to be unwarranted or invalid. How shall we en-

12. For a discussion of these ecclesiological dimensions, see Veli-Matti Kärkkäinen, *An Introduction to Ecclesiology* (Downers Grove, IL: InterVarsity, 2002).

13. D. P. Béchard, *The Scripture Documents: An Anthology of Official Catholic Teachings* (Collegeville, MN: Liturgical Press, 2002), 132.

14. 1 Cor 8:1-13; 10:23-31. See also Joyce S. Shin, "Accommodating the Other's Conscience: Saint Paul's Approach to Religious Tolerance," *Journal of the Society of Christian Ethics* 28 (2008): 3-23.

gage these situations? Scripture and tradition attest to the dialogical nature of living in a faith community. Arguments and debates appear everywhere in the history of theology and even in Scripture itself. So it is best to accept that constructive debate is an inevitable and healthy element in Christian living and in the human experience generally. The normative Christian approach to engaging interpretive differences should be one of love and civility, in which we recognize the "image of God" in each person and speak, to put it in canonical words, with "gentleness and respect" to believers and non-believers alike (1 Pet 3:15). The proper goals of the dialogue should be mutual understanding ("be quick to listen"), preservation of relationships ("pursue peace with all human beings," "love God and neighbor"), and a communal pursuit of the truth ("the truth shall set you free"). I take it that this describes, in a nutshell, a Christian understanding of how interpretive differences should be negotiated and discussed.

Having said this, are there occasions when we should set aside these basic rules of constructive, civil engagement and confront false or mistaken interpretations in a spirit of serious concern, incredulity, frustration, or anger? And are there situations when we should move even beyond this communicative action to what Habermas calls "strategic action," which sets aside any concern for mutual understanding and focuses instead on confronting and redressing the problems created by errant interpretation?[15] If the Bible and tradition are our guides then I believe that the answer to both questions must be "yes." But rarely is the situation as clear as it was in Nazi Germany, when Bonhoeffer and other Christians took bold action against an erring church. In life's more "mundane" circumstances, Christians will inevitably have different opinions concerning *when* such aggressive engagements would be warranted and also about *how* they should be conducted. These are weighty and much neglected ethical questions that I cannot address in detail.[16]

15. See Jürgen Habermas, *The Theory of Communicative Action* (2 vols.; Cambridge, UK: Polity Press, 1984-87).

16. For several texts that I find helpful, see Miroslav Volf, *Exclusion and Embrace: A Theological Exploration of Identity, Otherness, and Reconciliation* (Nashville: Abingdon, 1996); Samuel Wells, *Improvisation: The Drama of Christian Ethics* (Grand Rapids: Brazos, 2004). For a sensitive non-Christian perspective, see Edward Shils, *The Virtue of Civility: Selected Essays on Liberalism, Tradition, and Civil Society*, ed. S. Grosby (Indianapolis: Liberty Fund, 1997).

Final Thoughts

G od sanctifies and uses broken human beings to extend his grace to broken human beings. He uses me, and he uses you. And in doing so, though he cleanses us from sin, and though his Spirit is at work in us, he does not render us sinless, nor does he protect us from the foibles of errant judgment and the consequences of living in a fallen world. That he uses these "vessels of clay" for his purposes is remarkable but not wholly mysterious, for Paul tells us that he does so "that it may be made clear that this extraordinary power belongs to God and does not come from us" (2 Cor 4:7). In other words, there is a theological purpose behind God's choice to use human begins *as we are,* namely, so that the glory for redemption will truly be his.

The approach to Scripture that I have sketched here, and the doctrine of Scripture implicit in it, assumes that the same pattern which holds for humanity in general holds for the Bible's human authors. God sanctified broken human beings, finite and fallible though they were, and used them to convey his message of redemption in writing. The men involved (and perhaps a few women) included countless authors and editors, as well as those who were involved in the canonical processes that assembled Scripture.[1] In-

---

1. I have in mind the mother of King Lemuel (Prov 31:1), several songs in Scripture (Exodus 15 and Judges 5), and the woman or women who may have contributed to the Song of Songs.

sofar as they were human beings, they were no more perfect than we are, and in some cases — having lived even before the appearance of Christ — they probably knew less about theology and God's character than we know. But each contributed in ways conscious and unconscious to God's redemptive work, being selected by divine wisdom to provide a unique angle on God's unfolding plan and, hence, to serve as a distinctive voice for our spiritual nourishment.

The problem supposedly precipitated by this untidy situation is not as serious as it first appears. We might at first suppose that, as a result, there will be error and vice in Scripture, and that this will render it useless as a vehicle of grace and impugn God's character by association. While it is quite true that human error and vice do thereby insinuate themselves into Scripture, these human properties of Scripture, and of humanity and the cosmos generally, have no real bearing on God's goodness. Everything that is truly terrible in our world, and in us, can be traced back to human culpability. And all that is good and true — and all that is good and true in Scripture — is God's doing.

The "dark side" of Sacred Scripture is not something to disparage or belittle. It is evidence that our fallen condition is so serious that it warps not only the cosmos but even the written word itself. Nothing could say more clearly that we stand in need of Jesus Christ. Through his broken and resurrected body, everything is being healed. That *is* the good news.

Bibliography

Abraham, William J. *Canon and Criterion*. Oxford: Oxford University Press, 1998.

————. *Crossing the Threshold of Divine Revelation*. Grand Rapids: Eerdmans, 2006.

Adam, A. K. M. *Faithful Interpretation*. Minneapolis: Fortress, 2006.

Allert, Craig D. *A High View of Scripture? The Authority of the Bible and the Formation of the New Testament Canon*. Grand Rapids: Baker, 2007.

Allison, Dale C., Jr. *The Historical Christ and the Theological Jesus*. Grand Rapids: Eerdmans, 2009.

————. *The New Moses: A Matthean Typology*. Minneapolis: Fortress, 1993.

Anderson, Ray S. "The Resurrection of Jesus as Hermeneutical Criterion (Part I)." *TSF Bulletin* 9.1 (January-February, 1986): 9-15.

————. "The Resurrection of Jesus as Hermeneutical Criterion (Part II)." *TSF Bulletin* 9.2 (March-April, 1986): 15-22.

Aquinas, Thomas. *Summa Contra Gentiles*. Trans. J. F. Anderson. 3 vols. in 4. Notre Dame, IN: University of Notre Dame Press, 1975.

————. *Summa Theologica*. 5 vols. Allen, TX: Christian Classics, 1981.

Archer, Gleason L. *Encyclopedia of Bible Difficulties*. Grand Rapids: Zondervan, 1982.

Assmann, Jan. *The Mind of Egypt: History and Meaning in the Time of the Pharaohs*. New York: Metropolitan Books, 2002.

Aubert, Roger. *Vatican I*. Histoire des conciles oecuméniques 12. Paris: Éditions de l'Orante, 1964.

Augustine. *The Literal Meaning of Genesis*. Trans. J. H. Taylor. 2 vols. New York: Paulist, 1982.

Avalos, Hector. *Fighting Words: The Origins of Religious Violence*. Amherst, NY: Prometheus, 2005.

Bibliography

Barr, James. *Biblical Faith and Natural Theology*. Oxford: Clarendon, 1993.

―――. "Why the World Was Created in 4004 B.C.: Archbishop Ussher and Biblical Chronology." *Bulletin of the John Rylands Library* 67 (1985): 575-608.

Barth, Karl. *Church Dogmatics*. Edinburgh: T. & T. Clark, 1936-77.

―――. *The Epistle to Romans*. 6th ed. Oxford: Oxford University Press, 1968.

―――. *The Humanity of God*. Richmond: John Knox, 1960.

Barton, John. *Amos' Oracles against the Nations*. Cambridge: Cambridge University Press, 1980.

―――. "Natural Law and Poetic Justice in the Old Testament." *Journal of Theological Studies* 30 (1979): 1-14.

―――. *The Nature of Biblical Criticism*. Louisville: Westminster/John Knox, 2007.

―――. *People of the Book? The Authority of the Bible in Christianity*. Louisville: Westminster/John Knox, 1988.

Bauckham, Richard. *Bible and Mission: Christian Witness in a Postmodern World*. Grand Rapids: Baker Academic, 2003.

Baynes, Kenneth, James Bohman, and Thomas McCarthy, eds. *After Philosophy: End or Transformation?* Cambridge, MA: The MIT Press, 1987.

Béchard, D. P. *The Scripture Documents: An Anthology of Official Catholic Teachings*. Collegeville, MN: Liturgical, 2002.

Benin, Stephen D. *The Footprints of God: Divine Accommodation in Jewish and Christian Thought*. Albany: State University of New York Press, 1993.

Betti, Emilio. "Hermeneutics as the General Methodology of the Geisteswissenschaften." In G. Ormiston and A. Schrift, eds., *The Hermeneutic Tradition*. Albany, NY: SUNY Press, 1990. Pages 159-97.

Bigg, Charles. *A Critical and Exegetical Commentary on the Epistles of St. Peter and St. Jude*. ICC. Edinburgh: T. & T. Clark, 1969.

Billings, J. Todd. *The Word of God for the People of God: An Entryway to the Theological Interpretation of Scripture*. Grand Rapids: Eerdmans, 2010.

Bittar, E. Edward. *Bioethics*. Greenwich, CT: JAI, 1994.

Bonhoeffer, Dietrich. *Christ the Center*. Trans. E. H. Robertson. London: Harper and Row, 1978.

―――. *Ethics*. Trans. N. H. Smith. New York: Macmillan, 1955.

―――. *Reflections on the Bible: Human Word and Word of God*. Trans. M. E. Boring. Peabody, MA: Hendrickson, 2004.

Bowald, Mark Alan. *Rendering the Word in Theological Hermeneutics: Mapping Divine and Human Agency*. Burlington, VT: Ashgate, 2007.

Boyd, Gregory A. *Is God to Blame?* Downers Grove, IL: InterVarsity, 2003.

Boyer, Pascal. "Functional Origins of Religious Concepts: Ontological and Strategic Selection in Evolved Minds." *Journal of the Royal Anthropology Institute* 6 (2000): 195-214.

Boyer, Steven D. "The Logic of Mystery." *RelStud* 43 (2007): 89-102.

Buckley, James J., and David S. Yeago. "A Catholic and Evangelical Theology?" In J. J. Buckley and D. S. Yeago, eds., *Knowing the Triune God: The Work of the Spirit in the Practices of the Church.* Grand Rapids: Eerdmans, 2001. Pages 1-20.

Buggle, F. *Denn sie wissen nicht, was sie glauben, oder warum man redlicherweise nicht mehr Christ sein kann. Eine Streitschrift.* Reinbek: Rowohlt, 1992.

Burnett, Fred W. "Exposing the Anti-Jewish Ideology of Matthew's Implied Author: The Characterization of God as Father." In *Ideological Criticism of Biblical Texts.* Semeia 59. Atlanta: Scholars, 1993. Pages 155-91.

Calvin, John. *Commentaries on the First Book of Moses, called Genesis.* Trans. John King. 2 vols. Edinburgh: Calvin Translation Society, 1847-1850.

—————. *Institutes of the Christian Religion.* Trans. H. Beveridge. 2 vols. London: J. Clarke, 1949.

Caputo, John D. *Deconstruction in a Nutshell: A Conversation with Jacques Derrida.* New York: Fordham, 1997.

Catechism of the Catholic Church. Mahwah, NJ: Paulist, 1994.

Chapman, Stephen B. "Reclaiming Inspiration for the Bible." In C. G. Bartholomew et al., eds., *Canon and Biblical Interpretation.* Scripture and Hermeneutics Series 7. Grand Rapids: Zondervan, 2006. Pages 167-206.

Chesterton, G. K. *Orthodoxy.* Wheaton, IL: Harold Shaw, 1994.

Childs, Brevard S. *Introduction to the Old Testament as Scripture.* Philadelphia: Fortress, 1979.

Chrysostom, John. *On the Incomprehensible Nature of God.* Trans. P. W. Harkins. Fathers of the Church 34. Washington, DC: Catholic University of America, 1984.

Clarke, Thomas E. *The Eschatological Transformation of the Material World According to St. Augustine.* Woodstock, MD: Woodstock College Press, 1956.

Coggins, R. J. *Samaritans and Jews.* Atlanta: John Knox, 1975.

Collins, John J. "The Zeal of Phinehas: The Bible and the Legitimation of Violence." *Journal of Biblical Literature* 122 (2003): 3-21.

Cook, Michael J. "Confronting New Testament Attitudes on Jews and Judaism: Four Jewish Perspectives." *The Chicago Theological Seminary Register* 77 (1988): 3-30.

Copan, Paul. *Is God a Moral Monster? Making Sense of the Old Testament God.* Grand Rapids: Baker, 2011.

Craig, William Lane, and J. P. Moreland. *Philosophical Foundations for a Christian Worldview.* Downers Grove, IL: InterVarsity, 2003.

Cross, Frank Moore. *Canaanite Myth and Hebrew Epic: Essays in the History and the Religion of Israel.* Cambridge: Harvard University Press, 1973.

Davaney, Sheila Geeve. "Theology and the Turn to Cultural Analysis." In *Con-*

verging on Culture: Theologians in Dialogue with Cultural Analysis and Criticism. Oxford: Oxford University Press, 2001. Pages 3-16.

Davis, Ellen F. "Critical Traditioning: Seeking an Inner Biblical Hermeneutic." In Davis and Hays, eds., *The Art of Reading Scripture.* Pages 163-80.

Davis, Ellen F., and Richard B. Hays, eds. *The Art of Reading Scripture.* Grand Rapids: Eerdmans, 2003.

de Santillana, Giorgio. *The Crime of Galileo.* Chicago: University of Chicago Press, 1955.

Dulles, Avery Robert. *Models of Revelation.* Maryknoll, NY: Orbis, 1992.

Dunn, James D. G. *The Partings of the Ways between Christianity and Judaism and Their Significance for the Character of Christianity.* London: SCM; Philadelphia: Trinity, 1991.

Durkheim, Emil. *The Elementary Forms of the Religious Life.* Trans. K. E. Fields. New York: Free Press, 1995.

Earl, Douglas S. "The Christian Significance of Deuteronomy 7." *JTI* 3 (2009): 41-62.

———. *The Joshua Delusion? Rethinking Genocide in the Bible.* Eugene, OR: Cascade, 2010.

Eddy, Mary Baker. *Science and Health with Key to the Scriptures.* Boston: Stewart, 1912.

Ehrman, Bart D. *The Apostolic Fathers,* vol. 1. LCL 24. Cambridge: Harvard University Press, 2003.

———. *God's Problem: How the Bible Fails to Answer Our Most Important Question — Why We Suffer.* New York: HarperOne, 2008.

Eliade, Mircea. *A History of Religious Ideas.* 3 vols. Chicago: University of Chicago Press, 1978-85.

Elliott, J. K. *The Apocryphal New Testament.* Oxford: Clarendon, 1993.

Enns, Peter. *Inspiration and Incarnation: Evangelicals and the Problem of the Old Testament.* Grand Rapids: Baker Academic, 2005.

Fee, Gordon D. *The First Epistle to the Corinthians.* Grand Rapids: Eerdmans, 1987.

Ferguson, Everett. *Baptism in the Early Church: History, Theology, and Liturgy in the First Five Centuries.* Grand Rapids: Eerdmans, 2009.

Fine, Cordelia. "Is the Emotional Dog Wagging Its Rational Tail, or Chasing It?" *Philosophical Explorations* 9 (2006): 83-98.

Fitzmyer, Joseph A. *The Acts of the Apostles.* AB. New York: Doubleday, 1998.

———. *The Gospel According to Luke.* 2 vols. AB. Garden City, NY: Doubleday, 1985.

———. *The Interpretation of Scripture: In Defense of the Historical-Critical Method.* New York: Paulist, 2008.

Fowl, Stephen E. *Engaging Scripture: A Model for Theological Interpretation.* Malden, MA: Blackwell, 1998.

———. "The Importance of a Multivoiced Literal Sense of Scripture: The Example of Thomas Aquinas." In A. K. M. Adam, Stephen E. Fowl, Kevin J. Vanhoozer, and Francis Watson, *Reading Scripture with the Church*. Grand Rapids: Baker Academic, 2006. Pages 35-50.

—————. *Theological Interpretation of Scripture*. Eugene, OR: Cascade, 2009.

Franke, John R. *Manifold Witness: The Plurality of Truth*. Nashville: Abingdon, 2009.

Frei, Hans W. *The Eclipse of Biblical Narrative: A Study in Eighteenth and Nineteenth Century Hermeneutics*. New Haven: Yale University Press, 1974.

Geivett, R. Douglas. *Evil and the Evidence for God: The Challenge of John Hick's Theodicy*. Philadelphia: Temple University Press, 1993.

Gentner, Dedre, Keith J. Holyak, and Boicho N. Kokinov, eds. *The Analogical Mind: Perspectives from Cognitive Science*. Cambridge, MA: MIT Press, 2001.

Gorman, Michael J. *Elements of Biblical Exegesis*. Revised ed. Peabody, MA: Hendrickson, 2009.

Goulder, Michael D. *Midrash and Lection in Matthew*. London: SPCK, 1974.

Green, Joel B. "Acts of the Apostles." In R. P. Martin and P. H. Davids, eds., *Dictionary of the Later New Testament and Its Developments*. Downers Grove, IL: InterVarsity, 1997. Pages 7-24.

—————. *Seized by Truth: Reading the Bible as Scripture*. Nashville: Abingdon, 2007.

Green, William Henry. "Primeval Chronology: Are There Gaps in the Biblical Genealogies?" *BibSac* 47 (1890): 285-303.

Griffiths, J. G. *The Divine Verdict: A Study of Divine Judgment in the Ancient Religions*. Leiden: Brill, 1991.

Gundry, Robert. *Matthew: A Commentary on His Literary and Theological Art*. Grand Rapids: Eerdmans, 1982.

Gundry, Stanley N., ed. *Show Them No Mercy*. Grand Rapids: Zondervan, 2003.

Gunton, Colin E. *A Brief Theology of Revelation*. Edinburgh: T. & T. Clark, 1995.

—————. *Christ and Creation*. Grand Rapids: Eerdmans, 1992.

Habermas, Jürgen. *The Theory of Communicative Action*. 2 vols. Cambridge, UK: Polity, 1984-87.

Haidt, Jonathan. "The Emotional Dog and Its Rational Tail: A Social Intuitionist Approach to Moral Judgment." *Psychological Review* 108 (2001): 814-34.

Hahn, Scott W. *Covenant and Communion: The Biblical Theology of Pope Benedict XVI*. Grand Rapids: Brazos, 2009.

Hartranft, D., ed. *Corpus Schwenkfeldianorum*. Leipzig: Breitkopf und Härtel, 1907-61.

Hays, Richard B. "Can Narrative Criticism Recover the Theological Unity of Scripture?" *JTI* 2 (2008): 193-211.

—————. *The Moral Vision of the New Testament*. San Francisco: HarperCollins, 1996.

Heen, Erik M., and Philip D. W. Krey, eds. *Hebrews*. ACCS New Testament 10. Downers Grove, IL: InterVarsity, 2005.

Henry, Carl F. H. *God, Revelation, and Authority*. 6 vols. Waco, TX: Word, 1976-83.

Bibliography

Hirsch, E. D., Jr. *Validity in Interpretation*. New Haven: Yale, 1967.

Hitchens, Christopher. *God Is Not Great: How Religion Poisons Everything*. New York: Hachette, 2007.

Hofstadter, Douglas R. "Epilogue: Analogy as the Core of Cognition." In Gentner, Holyak, and Kokinov, eds., *The Analogical Mind*. Pages 499-538.

Holladay, William L. *The Psalms through Three Thousand Years: Prayerbook of a Cloud of Witnesses*. Minneapolis: Fortress, 1993.

Hunting, Claudine. "The Philosophes and Black Slavery." *Journal of the History of Ideas* 39 (1978): 405-18.

Iser, Wolfgang. *The Act of Reading: A Theory of Aesthetic Response*. Baltimore: Johns Hopkins University Press, 1980.

—————. *The Implied Reader: Patterns of Communication in Prose Fiction from Bunyan to Beckett*. Baltimore: Johns Hopkins University Press, 1974.

Jamieson-Drake, David W. *Scribes and Schools in Monarchic Judah: A Socio-Archaeological Approach*. Sheffield: JSOT, 1991.

Jeanrond, Werner. *Theological Hermeneutics: Development and Significance*. London: SCM, 1994.

Jeeves, Malcolm, and Warren S. Brown. *Neuroscience, Psychology, and Religion: Illusions, Delusion, and Realities about Human Nature*. West Conshohocken, PA: Templeton Foundation, 2009.

Johnson, Luke Timothy, and William S. Kurz, S.J. *The Future of Catholic Biblical Scholarship: A Constructive Conversation*. Grand Rapids: Eerdmans, 2002.

Jones, Scott J. *John Wesley's Conception and Use of Scripture*. Nashville: Abingdon, 1995.

Kärkkäinen, Veli-Matti. *An Introduction to Ecclesiology*. Downers Grove, IL: InterVarsity, 2002.

Kiernan, Ben. *Blood and Soil: A World History of Genocide and Extermination from Sparta to Darfur*. New Haven: Yale University Press, 2007.

Kuhn, Thomas S. *The Copernican Revolution*. Cambridge: Harvard University Press, 1957.

Kushner, Harold S. *When Bad Things Happen to Good People*. New York: Schocken, 1981.

Kysar, Robert. "John, the Gospel of." In D. N. Freedman, ed., *The Anchor Bible Dictionary*. New York: Doubleday, 1992. 6:912-31.

Lamb, David T. *God Behaving Badly: Is the God of the Old Testament Angry, Sexist and Racist?* Downers Grove, IL: InterVarsity, 2011.

Langford, Jerome J. *Galileo, Science, and the Church*. Revised ed. Ann Arbor: University of Michagan, 1971.

Lash, Nicholas. *Theology on the Way to Emmaus*. London: SCM, 1986.

Leithart, Peter J. *Deep Exegesis: The Mystery of Reading Scripture.* Waco: Baylor University Press, 2009.

Levering, Matthew. *Participatory Biblical Exegesis: A Theology of Biblical Interpretation.* Notre Dame, IN: University of Notre Dame Press, 2008.

Levinas, Emmanuel. *The Levinas Reader.* Seán Hand, ed. Oxford: Blackwell, 1989.

Lienhard, Joseph T. *Exodus, Leviticus, Numbers, Deuteronomy.* ACCS. Downers Grove, IL: InterVarsity, 2001.

Lierman, John. *The New Testament Moses: Christian Perceptions of Moses and Israel in the Setting of Jewish Religion.* WUNT² 173. Tübingen: Mohr Siebeck, 2004.

Lindars, Barnabas. *The Gospel of John.* NCBC. Grand Rapids: Eerdmans, 1972.

Lindbeck, George A. *The Nature of Doctrine.* Philadelphia: Westminster, 1984.

Lints, Richard. *The Fabric of Theology: A Prolegomenon to Evangelical Theology.* Grand Rapids: Eerdmans, 1993.

Lohfink, Norbert. "חרם *ḥāram.*" In G. J. Botterweck and H. Ringgren, eds., *Theological Dictionary of the Old Testament.* Grand Rapids: Eerdmans, 1974. 5:180-99.

Louth, Andrew. *Discerning the Mystery: An Essay on the Nature of Theology.* Oxford: Clarendon, 1990.

Luther, Martin. *Commentary on Romans.* Grand Rapids: Zondervan, 1954.

———. *Luther's Works.* F. Sherman, ed. 55 vols. Philadelphia: Fortress, 1971.

MacIntyre, Alasdair. *Whose Justice? Which Rationality?* Notre Dame, IN: University of Notre Dame Press, 1988.

Malherbe, Abraham J., and Everett Ferguson. *Gregory of Nyssa: The Life of Moses.* New York: Paulist, 1978.

Marshall, Bruce D. "Christ the End of Analogy." In T. J. White, ed. *The Analogy of Being: Invention of the Antichrist or Wisdom of God?* Grand Rapids: Eerdmans, 2011. Pages 280-313.

Marshall, I. Howard. *Beyond the Bible: Moving from Scripture to Theology.* Grand Rapids: Baker, 2004.

Martin, Dale B. *Pedagogy of the Bible: An Analysis and Proposal.* Louisville: Westminster/John Knox, 2008.

McFarland, Ian A. *In Adam's Fall: A Meditation on the Christian Doctrine of Original Sin.* Malden, MA: Wiley-Blackwell, 2010.

McGowan, A. T. B. *The Divine Authenticity of Scripture: Retrieving an Evangelical Heritage.* Downers Grove, IL: InterVarsity, 2007.

McKnight, Edgar V. "A Literary-Oriented Biblical Criticism." In *The Bible and the Reader: An Introduction to Literary Criticism.* Minneapolis: Fortress, 1985.

———. *Postmodern Use of the Bible: The Emergence of Reader-Oriented Criticism.* Nashville: Abingdon, 1988.

McKnight, Scot. "From Wheaton to Rome: Why Evangelicals Become Roman Catholic." *JETS* 45 (2002): 451-72.

Moberly, R. W. L. "What Is Theological Interpretation of Scripture?" *JTI* 3 (2009): 161-78.

Moreland, J. P. "Truth, Contemporary Philosophy and the Postmodern Turn." *JETS* 48 (2005): 77-88.

Nessan, Craig L. "Christian Faith in Dialogue with Darwin: Evolutionary Biology and the Meaning of the Fall." *Currents in Theology and Mission* 29 (2002): 85-93.

Newbigin, Lesslie. *The Gospel in a Pluralist Society.* Grand Rapids: Eerdmans, 1989.

———. *Proper Confidence: Faith, Doubt, and Certainty in Christian Discipleship.* Grand Rapids: Eerdmans, 1995.

Newman, John Henry. *A Grammar of Assent.* Garden City, NY: Doubleday, 1955.

Noll, Mark A., and Carol Nystrom. *Is the Reformation Over? An Evangelical Assessment of Contemporary Roman Catholicism.* Grand Rapids: Baker, 2005.

Nouwen, Henri J. M. *The Return of the Prodigal Son: A Meditation on Fathers, Brothers, and Sons.* New York: Doubleday, 1992.

O'Collins, Gerald. *Christology: A Biblical, Historical, and Systematic Study of Jesus.* Oxford: Oxford University Press, 1995.

O'Dowd, Ryan P. "A Chord of Three Strands: Epistemology in Job, Proverbs and Ecclesiastes." In M. Healy and R. Parry, eds., *The Bible and Epistemology: Biblical Soundings on the Knowledge of God.* Milton Keynes, UK: Paternoster, 2007. Pages 65-87.

Oden, Thomas C. *Systematic Theology.* 3 vols. Peabody: Prince, 1998.

Origen. *Homilies on Numbers.* Trans. T. P. Scheck. Downers Grove, IL: IVP Academic, 2009.

Owen, John. *The Death of Death in the Death of Christ.* London: Banner of Truth, 1963.

Pannenberg, Wolfhart. "The Doctrine of Creation and Modern Science." *Zygon* 23 (1988): 3-21.

———. *Systematic Theology.* 3 vols. Grand Rapids: Eerdmans, 1991-98.

Patte, Daniel M. *Ethics of Biblical Interpretation: A Reevaluation.* Louisville: Westminster/John Knox, 1995.

Pelikan, Jaroslav. *Acts.* Grand Rapids: Brazos, 2005.

———. *The Christian Tradition: A History of the Development of Doctrine.* 5 vols. Chicago: University of Chicago Press, 1971-89.

Placher, William C. *The Domestication of Transcendence.* Louisville: Westminster/John Knox, 1996.

Plantinga, Alvin. *God, Freedom, and Evil.* Grand Rapids: Eerdmans, 1977.

Plato. *The Republic.* Trans. P. Shorey. 2 vols.; LCL. Cambridge: Harvard University Press, 1942-43.

Polanyi, Michael. *Personal Knowledge: Towards a Post-Critical Philosophy.* London: Routledge, 1998.

———. *The Tacit Dimension.* Gloucester, MA: Peter Smith, 1983.

Polkinghorne, John. *Quarks, Chaos and Christianity*. 2d ed. New York: Crossroad, 2005.

Pope Benedict XVI. *Jesus of Nazareth: From the Baptism in the Jordan to the Transfiguration*. Trans. A. J. Walker. New York: Doubleday, 2007.

Radmacher, E. D., and R. D. Preus, eds. *Hermeneutics, Inerrancy and the Bible*. Grand Rapids: Zondervan, 1984.

Rahner, Karl. *Theological Investigations*, vol. 4. Trans. K. Smith. Baltimore: Helicon; London: Darton, Longman & Todd, 1974.

Ratzinger, Cardinal Joseph. "Biblical Interpretation in Conflict: On the Foundations and the Itinerary of Exegesis Today." In J. Granados et al., eds., *Opening Up the Scriptures: Joseph Ratzinger and the Foundations of Biblical Interpretation*. Grand Rapids: Eerdmans, 2008. Pages 1-29.

————. *In the Beginning: A Catholic Understanding of the Story of Creation and the Fall*. Grand Rapids: Eerdmans, 1995.

————. *The Nature and Mission of Theology: Approaches to Understanding Its Role in the Light of Present Controversy*. Trans. A. Walker. San Francisco: Ignatius, 1995.

————. *Truth and Tolerance: Christian Belief and World Religions*. Trans. H. Taylor. San Francisco: Ignatius, 2003.

Ratzinger, Cardinal Joseph, and Vittorio Messori. *The Ratzinger Report: An Exclusive Interview on the State of the Church*. Trans. S. Attanasio and G. Harrison. San Francisco: Ignatius, 1985.

Ricoeur, Paul. *Essays on Biblical Interpretation*. Philadelphia: Fortress, 1980.

————. *Oneself as Another*. Chicago: University of Chicago Press, 1992.

Rorty, Richard. *Philosophy and Social Hope*. New York: Penguin, 1999.

Rosenau, P. M. *Post-Modernism and the Social Sciences*. Princeton: Princeton University Press, 1992.

Roth, Martha T. *Law Collections from Mesopotamia and Asia Minor*. 2d ed; SBLWAW 6. Atlanta: Scholars, 1997.

Rowe, William L. "The Problem of Evil and Some Varieties of Atheism." *American Philosophical Quarterly* 16 (1979): 335-41.

————, ed. *God and the Problem of Evil*. Malden, MA: Blackwell, 2001.

Sanders, James A. *Canon and Community: A Guide to Canonical Criticism*. Philadelphia: Fortress, 1984.

Sandmel, Samuel. *Anti-Semitism in the New Testament?* Philadelphia: Fortress, 1978.

Santmire, H. Paul. *The Travail of Nature*. Philadelphia: Fortress, 1985.

Schniedewind, William M. *How the Bible Became a Book: The Textualization of Ancient Israel*. Cambridge: Cambridge University Press, 2004.

Seibert, Eric A. *Disturbing Divine Behavior: Troubling Old Testament Images of God*. Minneapolis: Fortress, 2009.

Seitz, Christopher R. "Canonical Approach." In G. B. Bartholomew et al., eds., *Dic-

tionary for Theological Interpretation of Scripture. Grand Rapids: Baker, 2005. Pages 100-102.

———. *Nicene Christianity: The Future for a New Ecumenism.* Grand Rapids: Brazos, 2001.

Shin, Joyce S. "Accommodating the Other's Conscience: Saint Paul's Approach to Religious Tolerance." *Journal of the Society of Christian Ethics* 28 (2008): 3-23.

Shuster, Marguerite. *The Fall and Sin: What We Have Become as Sinners.* Grand Rapids: Eerdmans, 2004.

Simon, Uriel. *Seek Peace and Pursue It: Topical Issues in the Light of the Bible: The Bible in the Light of Topical Issues.* Tel Aviv: Yediot Ahronot, 2002 (Hebrew).

Simonetti, Manlio, and Marco Conti, eds. *Job.* ACCS. Downers Grove, IL: InterVarsity, 2006.

Smith, Christian. *The Impossibility of Evangelical Biblicism.* Grand Rapids, MI: Brazos, 2011.

Smith, James K. A. *The Fall of Interpretation: Philosophical Foundations for a Creational Hermeneutics.* Downers Grove: InterVarsity, 2000.

Snaith, Norman H. The Book of Job: Its Origin and Purpose. SBT^2 11. London: SCM, 1968.

Snell, R. J. *Through a Glass Darkly: Bernard Lonergan and Richard Rorty on Knowing without a God's-Eye View.* Milwaukee: Marquette University Press, 2006.

Soggin, J. Alberto. *Introduction to the Old Testament.* Louisville: Westminster/John Knox, 1989.

Southgate, Christopher. *The Groaning of Creation: God, Evolution, and the Problem of Evil.* Louisville: Westminster/John Knox, 2008.

Sparks, Kenton L. *Ancient Texts for the Study of the Hebrew Bible: A Guide to the Background Literature.* Peabody, MA: Hendrickson, 2005.

———. *God's Word in Human Words: An Evangelical Appropriation of Critical Biblical Scholarship.* Grand Rapids: Baker, 2008.

———. "Gospel as Conquest: Mosaic Typology in Matthew 28:16-20." *CBQ* 68 (2006): 651-63.

Steinmetz, David C. "The Superiority of Pre-Critical Exegesis." *Theology Today* 37 (1980): 27-38.

Surin, Kenneth. *Theology and the Problem of Evil.* Oxford: Blackwell, 1986.

Swinburne, Richard. *The Coherence of Theism.* Oxford: Clarendon, 1997.

———. *Revelation: From Metaphor to Analogy.* Oxford: Clarendon, 1992.

Tamarin, Georges R. *The Israeli Dilemma: Essays on a Warfare State.* Rotterdam: University Press, 1973.

Thorsen, Donald A. D. *The Wesleyan Quadrilateral: Scripture, Reason and Experience as a Model of Evangelical Theology.* Grand Rapids: Zondervan, 1990.

Teilhard de Chardin, Pierre. *The Phenomenon of Man.* Trans. B. Wall. London: Collins, 1959.

Tigay, Jeffrey. *Deuteronomy.* Philadelphia: Jewish Publication Society, 1996.

Torrance, Alan J. "Can the Truth Be Learned? Redressing the 'Theologistic Fallacy' in Modern Biblical Scholarship." In M. Bockmuehl and A. J. Torrance, eds., *Scripture's Doctrine and Theology's Bible: How the New Testament Shapes Christian Dogmatics.* Grand Rapids: Baker, 2008. Pages 143-63.

Torrance, T. F. *Divine and Contingent Order.* Edinburgh: T. & T. Clark, 1981.

Trible, Phyllis. *Texts of Terror: Literary-Feminist Readings of Biblical Narratives.* New ed. London: SCM, 2002.

Vanhoozer, Kevin J. *The Drama of Doctrine: A Canonical Linguistic Approach to Christian Theology.* Louisville: Westminster/John Knox, 2005.

———. *Is There a Meaning in This Text? The Bible, The Reader, and the Morality of Literary Knowledge.* Grand Rapids: Zondervan, 1998.

van Inwagen, Peter. "Genesis and Evolution." In E. Stump, ed., *Reasoned Faith.* Ithaca, NY: Cornell University Press, 1993. Pages 93-127.

———. *The Problem of Evil.* Oxford: Clarendon, 2006.

Volf, Miroslav. *Captive to the Word of God: Engaging the Scriptures for Contemporary Theological Reflection.* Grand Rapids: Eerdmans, 2010.

———. *Exclusion and Embrace: A Theological Exploration of Identity, Otherness, and Reconciliation.* Nashville: Abingdon, 1996.

von Rad, Gerhard. *Genesis: A Commentary.* Revised ed. Philadelphia: Westminster, 1973.

———. *Wisdom in Israel.* London: SCM, 1972.

Wainwright, Geoffrey. *Is the Reformation Over? Catholics and Protestants at the Turn of the Millennia.* Milwaukee: Marquette University Press, 2000.

Ward, Keith. *What the Bible Really Teaches: A Challenge for Fundamentalists.* London: SPCK, 2004.

Ward, Timothy. *Words of Life: Scripture as the Living and Active Word of God.* Downers Grove: InterVarsity, 2009.

Watson, Francis. *Text and Truth: Redefining Biblical Theology.* Edinburgh: T. & T. Clark, 1997.

———. *Text, Church and World: Biblical Interpretation in Theological Perspective.* Grand Rapids: Eerdmans, 1994.

Webb, William J. *Slaves, Women, and Homosexuals: Exploring the Hermeneutics of Cultural Analysis.* Downers Grove, IL: InterVarsity, 2001.

Webster, John. *Holy Scripture: A Dogmatic Sketch.* Cambridge: Cambridge University Press, 2003.

Weinandy, Thomas G. *In the Likeness of Sinful Flesh: An Essay on the Humanity of Christ.* London; New York: T. & T. Clark, 2006.

Weinert, Friedel. *Copernicus, Darwin, and Freud: Revolutions in the History and Philosophy of Science*. Malden, MA: Wiley-Blackwell, 2009.

Wells, Samuel. *Improvisation: The Drama of Christian Ethics*. Grand Rapids: Brazos, 2004.

Wesley, John. *The Works of John Wesley*. 12 vols. London: Wesleyan Methodist Book Room, 1872.

Westerholm, Stephen. *Perspectives Old and New on Paul: The "Lutheran" Paul and His Critics*. Grand Rapids: Eerdmans, 2004.

Westphal, Merold. *Overcoming Onto-Theology: Toward a Postmodern Christian Faith*. New York: Fordham University Press, 2001.

———. "Post-Kantian Reflections on the Importance of Hermeneutics." In R. Lundin, ed., *Disciplining Hermeneutics: Interpretation in Christian Perspective*. Grand Rapids: Eerdmans, 1997. Pages 57-66.

———. *Whose Community? Which Interpretation?* Grand Rapids: Baker, 2009.

White, A. D. *The History of the Warfare of Science with Theology in Christendom*. 2 vols. New York: Appleton, 1920.

Williams, D. H. *Evangelicals and Tradition: The Formative Influence of the Early Church*. Grand Rapids: Baker, 2005.

Witherington, Ben, III. *The Jesus Quest: The Third Search for the Jew of Nazareth*. Downers Grove, IL: InterVarsity, 1997.

Wittgenstein, Ludwig. *Philosophical Investigations*. Trans. G. E. M. Anscombe. Oxford: Blackwell, 1953.

Wolterstorff, Nicholas. *Divine Discourse: Philosophical Reflections on the Claim that God Speaks*. Cambridge: Cambridge University Press, 1995.

———. *Justice: Rights and Wrongs*. Princeton: Princeton University Press, 2008.

Wood, W. Jay. *Epistemology: Becoming Intellectually Virtuous*. Downers Grove, IL: InterVarsity, 1998.

Work, Telford. *Living and Active: Scripture in the Economy of Salvation*. Grand Rapids: Eerdmans, 2002.

Worthington, Everett L. *Coming to Peace with Psychology*. Downers Grove: InterVarsity, 2010.

Wright, N. T. *The Last Word: Beyond the Bible Wars to a New Understanding of the Authority of Scripture*. San Francisco: HarperCollins, 2005.

Wuthnow, Robert. *Acts of Compassion: Caring for Others and Helping Ourselves*. Princeton: Princeton University Press, 1991.

Yarchin, William. *History of Biblical Interpretation*. Peabody, MA: Hendrickson, 2004.

Yeago, David S. "The New Testament and the Nicene Dogma: A Contribution to the Recovery of Theological Exegesis." *Pro Ecclesia* 3 (1994): 152-64.

Young, Frances M. *Biblical Exegesis and the Formation of Christian Culture*. Cambridge, UK: Cambridge University Press, 1997.

Ziesler, John. *Paul's Letter to the Romans*. London: SCM, 1989.

Zimmerman, Jens. *Recovering Theological Hermeneutics: An Incarnational-Trinitarian Theory of Interpretation*. Grand Rapids: Baker, 2004.

Index of Authors

Index of Subjects

Accommodation, 24, 53-55, 68
Adam (biblical figure), 36
Adoption (in Scripture), 55
Adoptionism (Christology), 23
Allegory, 41, 95, 141, 149, 151
Analogy, 81, 84, 134, 142, 150, 152
Antirealism, 74, 76, 77, 78, 81
Arianism, 24
Aristotle, 92
Assumption of Moses, 36
Athanasius, 23, 24
Audience. *See* Implied Audience, Real
  Audience
Augustine, 17-18, 36, 48, 50, 57, 68, 74,
  88, 91, 93, 95, 98, 108, 120, 122, 136,
  141, 151-52
Auschwitz, 14, 19
Author. *See* Authorial Intention, Im-
  plied Author, Real Author
Authorial Intention, 94, 97, 99

Bhagavad-Gita, 61
Biblicism, 29, 138

Calvin, John, 15, 33-34, 39, 50, 53, 95
Canaanites, 38, 45, 111, 112, 147-48
Catholicism, 35, 37, 46, 89, 125-27, 130,
  153

Chalcedon, Definition of, 89
Christian Science, 15, 43
Christological Interpretation, 109
Christology, 23
Chrysostom, John, 15, 108, 133
Clement of Alexandria, 57
Community (role in interpretation), 153
Conscience, 154
Copernicus, Nicolaus, 5
Creeds, 127-28, 153

David (biblical figure), 30, 31, 35, 94
Diversity (theological), 35, 38-44, 49, 67,
  103-4, 106, 110
Docetism, 23, 24, 27

Eastern Orthodoxy, 35, 89, 125-27, 153
Eddy, Mary Baker, 15
Eliphaz (biblical figure), 120
Elisha (biblical figure), 153
Enlightenment, 75, 115
Enoch, 36
Epistemology, 72, 86
Experience, 118, 129

Fall (doctrine of), 15, 86
Fourfold Sense (of Scripture), 149
Fundamentalism, 64, 76, 138

175

Index of Scripture References